What people are

Be Nir

The key to the success of any business is the effectiveness of the management team, a truth proven repeatedly over my thirty-year investment career. Having worked closely with Marty Strong as the leading investor and chairman of his board of directors, I can attest to Marty living his *Be Nimble* principles every day. As a strategic thinker, he transformed a small, acquired healthcare company into a rapidly growing market segment leader. His talent at organizational design allowed the team to scale up operations to deliver higher quality medical services. He is a dynamic business leader, put simply, Marty leads by example and is a high-performance innovator. *Be Nimble* will be required reading for all our portfolio company executives.
William Hayes, Investment professional with over thirty years of experience and Co-founder, partner of private equity firm Mosaic Capital Partners

Be Nimble, How the Navy SEAL Mindset Wins on the Battlefield and in Business, is a testimony of leadership and success written by an effective, well-respected Navy SEAL officer and world-class business leader. The book is full of brilliant ideas and provides a straightforward approach to decision-making that can be employed regardless of personal or business objectives. Marty Strong's vision, his strength of purpose, and his focus are on point. He provides the reader with a rare opportunity to access proven advice, unlike anything available in the conventional business world, that can be utilized by any person or organization approaching significant challenges and/or when building strong and effective teams.
Don Mann, New York Times bestselling author of *Inside SEAL Team SIX,* and author of *Reaching Beyond Boundaries: A Navy SEAL's Guide to Achieving Everything You've Ever Imagined*

For forty years, both in the SEAL Teams and in business, I've marveled at how Marty Strong's adaptive mindset could cut through the fog of distractors to identify the real challenges we were facing. I often observed his asymmetrical thinking kicking in, providing us razor sharp focus, and allowing us to crystalize a workable solution. Time after time, his creative energy and leadership produced the WIN-WIN outcome we were all seeking. I can remember saying to myself, "Why hadn't I thought of that?" For decision-makers, *Be Nimble, How the Navy SEAL Mindset Wins on the Battlefield and in Business,* will give you and your team the keys to the same innovative, strategic insight that marked Marty's leadership and selfless success both in the SEAL Teams and in business.

Thomas Steffens, Rear Admiral (retired SEAL)
Former Commodore Naval Special Warfare Group Four
Former Commander Naval Special Warfare Center

Be Nimble

How the Creative Navy SEAL Mindset Wins on the Battlefield and in Business

Be Nimble

How the Creative Navy SEAL Mindset Wins on the Battlefield and in Business

Marty Strong
CEO and Chief Strategy Officer
Retired Navy SEAL Officer and Combat Veteran
BBA, MA, Lean Six Sigma Master Blackbelt

Winchester, UK
Washington, USA

First published by Business Books, 2021
Business Books is an imprint of John Hunt Publishing Ltd., No. 3 East St., Alresford, Hampshire SO24 9EE, UK
office@jhpbooks.com
www.johnhuntpublishing.com
www.johnhuntpublishing.com/business-books

For distributor details and how to order please visit the 'Ordering' section on our website.

ISBN: 978 1 78904 840 7
978 1 78904 841 4 (ebook)
Library of Congress Control Number: 2020951027

A CIP catalogue record for this book is available from the British Library.

Design: Stuart Davies

UK: Printed and bound by CPI Group (UK) Ltd, Croydon, CR0 4YY
Printed in North America by CPI GPS partners

Contents

Preface

Everything today is changing, evolving at hyper speed when compared to earlier generations, and *it isn't going to slow down.* Technology is a part of it, but social, political, and spiritual changes are also contributing to a sense of helplessness for many people. If you are not a leader, you feel like a victim. You observe and experience events without the ability or knowledge to influence events and stop the madness. If you are a leader, you are overwhelmed. You lack the resources to cope, and you find you're always three steps behind the solution.

You know deep down there must be a better way to deal with the chaos, the confusion, the crazy, and you're right. This book is about business leadership, but its message extends to any leader or aspiring leader of any organization. There is a better way. I began as a child who didn't *try* to be agile, nimble, or creative, I just was. I was also open minded and curious. We all began life with the tools to be creative, to succeed. It's time to apply that essential childlike freedom of thought and action to the all too serious business of leadership. Are you with me?

Forward

A submarine at sea under "normal" conditions, is world of its own, and, by any standard, a challenging, crowded habitat. A built-in shortage of bunks mandates a fourth of the crew "hot bunk". Sailor A crawls out of a bunk and goes on watch, relieving Sailor B. Sailor B grabs a little chow and then crawls into that same bunk, maybe still warm from Sailor A – Voila: Hot Bunking. That's "normal" life on a fast attack submarine.

To survive and thrive inside such close quarters – a thirty-foot-wide by two-hundred-foot-long steel cylinder, is difficult. Operating submerged for weeks or months at a time in an unforgiving environment, the dark ocean depths, was no picnic either. It was an unforgiving world below the surface, a place where you don't make the same mistake twice and live to tell about it.

Submarine sailors live by a strict ethos. Simply put, this ethos is: 1. Follow the procedure; 2. Supervise everything; and 3. Communicate clearly. Submariners earn their right to be part of this culture through a rigorous one year on board qualification process (which follows extensive shore based training) culminating in a "Dolphin Ceremony" wherein the former non-qualified sailor is officially designated, Qualified in Submarines, and pinned with the coveted Submarine Dolphin uniform insignia.

Many groups in the Navy lay claim to an elite military heritage, fighter pilots for one, submariners do also. But the one naval warfare group that pilots and submariners would readily acknowledge as special are the United States Navy SEALs. These unique men who proudly wear the golden eagle insignia, fiercely clutching a flintlock pistol and Neptune's trident in its talons. The SEAL's insignia is fondly referred to as the "Trident" and it says all that needs to be said about the man wearing it.

Submariners and SEALs, two elite groups; both believe they have no equal, both possess a unique culture, intolerant of outsiders. Now bring these warriors together. Tell the submariners, "Those THIRTY-TWO additional bodies on your ship will make the Hot-bunking, well, HOTTER. SEALs – not qualified submariners – will be breathing YOUR oxygen, eating YOUR food, taking up the precious few seats in YOUR crew's mess on movie night and causing you to wait even longer for a bathroom break, a shower or a cup of coffee. Add to this the news that You are no longer the front line against maritime aggression the world over. Your mission now, is to deliver the SEALs and their mini submarine to their target launch point.

What about those elite SEALs? They'll be living, cohabitating with a surly crew of displaced professionals, inside an already jam-packed submarine. A place where your elite SEAL skills have no value. If something goes wrong, you need to get out of the way. Of course, SEALs are always in the way on a submarine. They wait, plan, workout, eat, sleep and repeat. They wait patiently for that moment when finally, they are given the orders to go. And while the SEALs leave the submarine on their way to fame and glory, those submarine sailors are grumbling. It *feels* like they've been reduced to highly qualified bus drivers.

What's a submarine skipper to do? I know what I did in this tenuous predicament. I enlisted the leadership skills and prowess of a miracle worker – Lieutenant Marty Strong, the SEAL Delivery Team Task Unit Commander assigned to my fast attack submarine for six months overseas. I'm convinced no other SEAL leader I've worked with, before or after, could've created the harmony, cohesiveness, and common sense of shared mission purpose among all of us, as Marty Strong did in those six months.

Marty was acutely aware of the problems heightened egos might cause and from the very beginning of our relationship, strived to eliminate that potential issue. Marty's leadership prowess influenced both his SEALs and my submariners, to dispense with self-aggrandizing bravado. He sponsored sports events, tours, firing range experiences. He did everything needed to establish a great comradery, even before we began our six-month deployment. We became two highly specialized naval warfare groups fused into one extraordinarily successful mission team. It was indeed an amazing thing for me to watch.

It was fortunate for me that he was the SEAL Task Unit Commander chosen by the SEAL community to work with me and my submarine crew. Officially and by rank, I was his direct superior, his BOSS at sea; I was the senior person responsible for our combined overall mission success – either we submariners and SEALs succeeded together, as one team, or we failed together. But I quickly learned that Lieutenant Strong didn't require my sage guidance. He was fully capable of leading all aspects, from mission execution and planning, to preparation, post mission assessment, and debrief. Together we were a highly successful leadership team, and together we melded our two populations of special characters into a tight unit.

Be Nimble is a book about REAL LEADERSHIP; leadership behaviors, attitudes, techniques, and skills developed and honed on the front lines. Those front lines for Marty were in high school, sports, combat, the ocean depths, business, national media, counterterrorism, and family life – these are all places where a leader is needed, but not always present.

The pressures and stresses of these situations tend to drive people to a reassessment of who they are and what matters to them. In *Crucibles of Leadership*, Harvard Business Review refers to such situations as times when leaders examine their values, question their assumptions, and hone their judgement. They emerge from the crucible stronger and surer of themselves and their purpose – fundamentally changed. If you want to fundamentally change your leadership approach, *Be Nimble, How the Navy SEAL Mindset Wins on the Battlefield and in Business,* will transform you.

Brad McDonald, Captain, U.S. Navy, Retired, Former Commanding Officer of the SEAL capable STURGEON Class attack submarine, USS L. MENDEL RIVERS, and author of *The Art and Skill of Sales Psychology*

Acknowledgements

Any collection of serious thoughts and ideas regarding leadership should be tested and challenged before going to print. *Be Nimble* wouldn't have been written without the loving support and tolerance of my loving wife, Michele. I must also thank my manuscript review team of eight, highly intelligent, experienced, business owners and executives, chief among them, Charles Rushworth, Colonel, United States Marine Corps, retired. They read every word, without complaint, and generously offered their keen and candid insight. Without them, the book would be far less valuable.

Chapter One

My Leadership Journey

"It is not the strongest of the species that survives, nor the most intelligent, but the one most responsive to change."
Charles Darwin

I've been many things in my life, but so far, I have not held an academic position teaching leadership, at least, not outside the Navy. That's right. I decided to write a book about leaders, for leaders, without the "required" conventional academic credentials, that carry with them the expectation of actionable value and insight.

I've read hundreds of these books and confess that the more experience I gained in actual leadership functions, the less those institutional books inspired growth. I realized they were speaking to large corporations, multi-tiered behemoths, not most leaders like me who were swinging away in small or mid-sized companies, startups, and rescues. You know what? That's okay. It was time to speak to the masses, not the elites living high at the top of the corporate organizational chart. It was time for me to impart my frustration with the status quo in leadership education and to reveal what I've learned by actually *leading*.

In *Be Nimble, How the Navy SEAL Mindset Wins on the Battlefield and in Business,* I've applied lessons learned personally or through close observation, in the trenches, under fire, both in uniform and as a business professional. So, if you are wondering why you should listen to anything this guy has to say, I'll respond this way. My story is real, and my leadership experiences are real. You won't be sorry you made the investment in time, the investment in yourself. Becoming a nimble leader is a journey, but trust me, it is a journey worth the effort.

I was born in the western panhandle of Nebraska, the oldest of three children raised by two depression era Iowa farmers. My dad Chet and my mom Barb were polar opposites. Dad was a non-verbal disciplinarian, a stickler for perfection and execution in a flat top haircut. My mother, on the other hand, was a dreamer, funny and chatty to the extreme. She wore her hair piled high, emulating movie stars of the day. Dad loved history, war movies and mom. Mom loved Dean Martin, Frank Sinatra, and Dad. Don't ask me why these two extremes in personality became husband and wife, but they did have one thing in common, they both loved to read.

It was my parents shared love of reading that at the age of four thrust me head long into exciting stories of Vikings and pirates, and not so exciting books about physicists and great artists (I'll let you guess who influenced me to read what subject). My earliest memories are of sitting by myself, book in hand, ignoring the world as I consumed every book, I could get my hands on. Oddly, I don't remember many of the fun books my mom gave me to read. She was happy just to see me happy.

Don't get me wrong, I wasn't so fixated on books that I ignored life and life in rural Nebraska was all about role playing. My friends and I were pushed outside by our parents who believed kids should be playing not sitting around. We accommodated that philosophy by riding bikes, too far, too fast, and down hills that were too steep.

We played soldier, spaceman, cowboys, we pretended to be superheroes or monsters. In the summer we built forts, dug tunnels, and followed the local streams catching crawdads and frogs. During the winter we organized snow wars, creating forts out of ploughed snow heaped ten feet high. We tunneled inside, punched out observation ports, and then poured water on the outside walls, making the structure impervious to snowballs.

It was fun being a kid. We were creative, imaginative, and willing to try anything. Attributes I would later in life ascribe to the art of being nimble. We all start out nimble, but the world has a way or pounding us into an acceptable mold. My dad was no exception. As I grew older my dad required me to deliver a detailed breakdown of each book I read while he asked questions and accepted or rejected my observations and conclusions.

If I was lucky enough to hit all the high points my reward was another book. Luckily for me, it seemed my dad had an endless supply, but it wasn't all bad. I've had years to reflect on the impact of both my parents and I think the strange mix of my mom's love of fantasy, science fiction, and adventure, and my dad's practical approach to self-learning and the consumption of knowledge, created in me a healthy balance. A love for creativity and a love for performance and achievement.

When I was ten years old my dad brought us all together and announced we were moving to Japan! I loved the idea, my mom, not so much. Their marriage lasted the four years we spent in Japan and ended with my siblings and I back in Nebraska with our mom. I was fourteen and confused. It got worse. My mom was soon diagnosed with schizophrenia and manic depression. She'd become an alcoholic while in Japan and that complicated her other illnesses. For the next year and a half, I assumed the role of family patriarch.

Like any teenager I had things I wanted to accomplish, get a car, a girlfriend, make the football team, you know the list. I was able to work odd jobs to save money and eventually I bought an old car. Then I made the Varsity football team, but the illusive girlfriend thing was both expensive and time consuming. When I wasn't working two jobs or at football practice, I was trying to hold our family together. My mother and I didn't see eye to eye on much of anything in those days. She spent time in and out of institutions and I pretended to be normal. My friends and the neighbors were sympathetic, but it was a lonely existence. More often than not, I escaped by reading.

A month after turning sixteen my world flipped upside

down. My mom was dating a guy who decided it was okay to smack my little brother around. When I found out I went on the warpath, demanding that my mom tell me who this guy was so I could seek my revenge, all one hundred and twenty-five pounds of me. My mom blew a brain gasket and started chasing me around with a butcher knife. I ran to my room (shared with my brother) stuffed as much as I could into a pillowcase and paused long enough to say goodbye to him. Once out of the second-floor apartment window I ran down to a pay phone and called a friend. The next day I was on a plane bound for Honolulu, Hawaii to live with my dad.

I appreciated that my dad was willing to rescue me, but as it turned out, he'd started a new life. He was married again, and the new Mrs. Strong wasn't too happy having a lanky teenager roaming around their home. I found that my dad had loosened up a bit. He was sporting long hair and facial hair, gone was the military look. He was so different I nearly missed finding him in the airport when I arrived. He'd mellowed a little too, but one thing hadn't changed, I was going to be studying.

My dad knew it would be hard for me to make friends and get a job. Having a car in Waikiki wasn't practical, everything was walking distance and the city had a great bus system. His solution for my poverty was, you guessed it, reading for dollars. He still had his personal library and it had grown. He started me with the great religions, the Bible, the Koran, the book of Mormon, Buddhism, and the Hindu Upanishads. One book at a time, one religion at a time. The payoff was thirty bucks! All I had to do was read the books, brief him on the content, and cha-ching, pocket change!

I'd slacked off reading serious books while living in Nebraska, focusing mostly on escapist novels. Now I was going to school and learning at home, too. My dad was still unemotional, but he never assumed I couldn't handle the challenging material. This eventually led me to believe I could tackle any subject by reading about it in a book. I didn't know it at the time, but the discipline and the wide range of exposure, was shaping the way I looked at the world, and at problems. This discipline and world view would come in handy later.

My time in Hawaii was also a time of emotional growth for me. This was my fourth move since the age of ten. I realized I was becoming proficient at compartmentalizing negative inputs and even better at focusing on the future. I thought about the future a lot. This was the beginning of my strength in forecasting outcomes. Much of this skill came from a deepening understanding of history and the lessons it held for the future. It was also influenced by my love of fantasy and science fiction literature. My personal resilience and ability to compartmentalize pain and negative inputs became a part of my personality by the time I left Hawaii for Detroit, Michigan.

My senior year in Grosse Point, Michigan, a suburb of Detroit, was uneventful but for one life changing event. I was a stellar student and carried a near 4.0 GPA every year of high school. My constant moving was both a curse and a blessing. Every school system rejected much of the work associated with the last school system. The result was four years packed with core courses. The forced home schooling only added to my academic abilities.

Being a great student didn't impress my dad. He was doing well in the world, a senior government employee in the Department of Defense. He could have encouraged me to go to college, but he didn't. In fact, he refused to pay a dime of my college costs if I decided on my own to attend a school. His guidance was simple and to the point, see the world, grow up some more, join the Navy. So, without many options I did what he suggested, I joined up. I hit Bootcamp at the ripe old age of 17. Bootcamp wasn't hard, but I was exposed to a crazy variety of Americans. Texans, Latinos, inner city gangsters, smooth talkers from the Gulf states, and New Yorkers.

After completing Navy bootcamp, I went straight to the Navy's RADAR and air traffic control school. I graduated 17 weeks later and was scheduled to go to a Navy Cruiser in the Mediterranean Sea, that's when fate stepped in. Through a mix-up in orders I have never been able to understand, I found myself one week later standing with one hundred and twenty-six other young men, all sporting shaved heads. I was in Coronado, California, home of the elite U.S. Navy SEALs and the location of Basic Underwater Demolition/SEAL training known as BUD/S.

I'd tried to talk to anybody who would listen. It was a mistake. I was supposed to be a RADAR expert on a ship. I told them I wasn't the superhero type. I was five foot nine and one hundred and twenty-eight pounds soaking wet, they agreed. In the end it didn't matter, nobody listened. I was told by a grizzled old Vietnam veteran that they were called orders for a reason. I gave up, it was day one, of week one, of the toughest military training in the world. At the time. the twenty-six-week course was a meat grinder. Statistically, only twenty-five percent graduated from the daunting experience and the instructors frequently reminded us of this fact. I did the math, thirty-one. Only thirty-one of the horde of would-be warriors in my class would graduate. Little did I know at the time that we'd only graduate thirteen of the original student body, and that I'd be one of them.

Becoming a Navy SEAL was difficult and exhilarating at the same time. I recognized early on that my strange upbringing had contributed to my success in the elite program. My abilities to compartmentalize and stay optimistic about the future in the face of early teenage adversity was a prescription for success in the SEAL teams. I worked hard to learn the fighting skills and the planning skills. SEALs were thinking warriors. To get into the SEAL program you must have a high IQ and score in the top five percent of all Navy candidates in the Navy's general aptitude test. I was smart, but so was everybody else.

My understanding of military history and my ability to see the big picture resulted in my being assigned to officers putting together mission plans. I loved working all the puzzles, logistics, intelligence analysis, and planning our actions. This continual drill, year after year, trained me to project manage men and equipment, consumables such as food, water, and fuel.

By the time I was twenty-three I had packed on fifteen pounds of new muscle and advanced in the ranks to my first position of leadership. I will tell you this early leadership assignment did not go well. I made every mistake in the book and probably some they added to that book later. Straight forward positional authority comes with every title, but SEALs don't respect titles, they respect leaders.

I absorbed these hard lessons, took my lumps, and grew professionally. At the age of twenty-five, I became the youngest person to be promoted to Chief Petty Officer in the United States Navy. I learned new, tough lessons at this level of leadership and became successful enough to be selected for officer candidate school two years later.

Along the way I'd acquired a bachelor's degree in business administration and found the information nearly useless in a leadership role. The business school taught management. Managers manage things and people through processes and systems. I'd learned as a young SEAL that leaders need to lead when processes and systems break down or become obsolete. My degree had missed the mark. I tucked this lesson away for another time, my days in the Navy were coming to an end.

After twenty exciting years in the Navy SEAL Teams, I hung up my fins and became a civilian. Twenty years, ten as an enlisted SEAL, and another ten as an officer, had taken its toll on me physically. The SEAL teams are much like professional sports league. You start out in elite physical condition and then the job begins to chip away at you, one injury at a time.

I'd led thirty-six successful special operations combat missions in my twenty-year career and hadn't suffered so much as a scratch from contact with an enemy of my country. Yet, I was rated with several disabilities as I walked out the door. Parachute accidents, armored vehicle crashes, falling off any number of things – repeatedly, and suffering thousands of hours bouncing up and down in small boats. At the end of twenty years I was done. What would be next?

I'd finished my graduate degree in management before retiring and looked forward to applying that knowledge in business. My first job out of uniform was with an investment firm, Legg Mason, Wood Walker. The first day at work was a rude awakening to the truth many learn the hard way, your college education isn't experience. It turned out neither was knowing how to blow up a bridge. I was a new guy all over again. I took inventory. I didn't know how to sell, create a personal brand, market my personal brand, or perform the subtle skills of a consultant. I loved the idea of being a financial advisor but didn't know how to start. I was bluntly told that the secret to success was to go out and find clients.

I spent a day in denial, shook off the feeling of dread, then got to work. Cold calling for hours, cold walking for weeks at a time, seminars, booths at major local events, and I studied. Not textbooks, people. SEALs were pretty much cut from the same cloth. Witty, tough, highly intelligent, they were able to accept adverse circumstances and figure out a way forward. I found out quickly that normal people were different. They needed assurance, guidance, and hope. They needed someone to lean on for strength, so I became that person.

I was back in a leadership role. The job was twenty-five percent analytics, twenty-five percent investing and fifty percent coaching, mentoring, and inspiring clients. So, in a strange way I excelled at my new profession by eventually applying my core leadership experience from my prior profession. Oh, did

I already mention my college education credentials were of no use?

After seven years I had a thriving business. Financial services firms often set you up under their label and provide the backroom support while taking a percentage of your sales. It took me twenty months to match my annual compensation as an officer in the SEAL teams. No base salary, all commissions, and fees. After the first two years I moved my book of clients to UBS, the United Bank of Switzerland. They were the largest financial services company in the world at the time and I'd found a home. I became an Account Vice President and Portfolio Manager. I'd arrived. Then as it often did in my life, fate stepped in yet again.

America was attacked on September 11, 2001 while I sat in a regional manager's office discussing market share. He had his television on in the corner of the room with the sound turned off. I found out about the plane strikes when a woman broke into our meeting declaring the financial offices in the world trade towers were on fire. The manager looked over my shoulder at the television and I turned around. That was it. Fate.

I left the business of making money for other people a few months after the attack in New York and Washington D.C. and became a counterterrorism consultant. It was an easy choice. I wanted to get into the fight, I could envision the SEAL Teams, men I knew well, spinning up, staging, and planning. It was driving me crazy, but I found my service-connected disabilities prevented me from putting on a uniform again. The next best thing was to defend the homeland.

For the next few years, I provided insights to the federal government and to major defense firms gearing up for the war. I helped security planners envision potential attacks, showed them their vulnerabilities, and aided in hardening soft targets. It wasn't combat but it was something, I was contributing the only way I knew how.

The work was rewarding and instructional. I honed my

writing and speaking skills to a sharp edge as a consultant, briefing senior leaders and corporate officers. I was also successful financially but that wasn't what drove me on each day. I knew myself and other retired military and law enforcement experts were working as fast as possible to prevent another terrorist attack. In time, the war didn't end, and I eventually closed up my consulting practice and joined a midsized defense company. This company would rapidly expand into a billion-dollar, worldwide operation.

I started out small. I was assigned to lead a department initially consisting of fifty to sixty people. Now, for the first time in over a decade since completing my graduate studies, I was finally able to apply my business school, book learning. I evaluated existing systems and processes. Canvassed the talent and reorganized. It was hard, different than UBS or consulting. I now had direct reports, employees and with this responsibility came challenges.

Four years later I was a senior vice president and responsible for much more. I learned how to grow a department into a division, and a division, into a separate company. I learned how to lead people who worked remotely, all over the planet, and I learned that finally, my business education had paid off. However, the most important lesson I learned during this period was that there was a distinct difference between leadership and management, especially in times of crisis. I had performed in both roles and was ready for something new.

In 2009 I joined a small defense company founded by a friend and former SEAL. It was a new challenge, one that allowed me to have an equity ownership stake in our success. I'd watched an agile, adaptive young company, grow into a stumbling billion dollar a year bureaucracy (although at the time I didn't appreciate the valuable lessons I'd been exposed to). My new challenge was straightforward, grow or die.

And grow we did. From one company into five companies

over the next five years. My partner and I sold the business to the employees, a process referred to as an ESOP, and I stayed on as Chief Executive Officer and Chief Strategy Officer. The focus of three of our five companies is healthcare. It's a dynamic and continually changing industry that demands attention and innovation. It isn't easy, and I don't always make the right decisions, but I go to work every day with a smile on my face, leadership has finally become fun.

I've completed my share of training and education, mostly in military leadership or business management. I've watched leaders, listened to leaders, followed leaders (good ones, not so good ones, and terrible ones), and I've been a practicing leader for over forty years. I've tried to find books or courses that hit the right themes, pushed the right hot buttons, you know – experiences developed by real leaders, focused on actual leading, in the trenches, on the factory floor, or in the board room. Alas, these works, and courses are difficult to find. So, after reading far too many books about general management principles I decided to right down my formula for leadership success.

If you are a leader, want to be a leader, or want to understand how good leaders think and influence success, this book is for you! I truly believe you can learn to be a leader and if you are already one, you can learn to be a better leader. I've made the learning process in *Be Nimble* progressive on purpose, a series of tools, tips, insights, and ideas that build, one upon the other. I believe you'll understand and appreciate the logic of this approach as you move through the material.

Chapter Two

Are You Ready?

"It is unwise to be too sure of one's own wisdom."
Mahatma Gandhi

In the SEALs there was a saying (fair warning, there are a ton of sayings in the SEAL teams), when war finally comes, you will go into battle with whatever skill and knowledge you possess at that time. In other words, you can't get the time back you wasted before you are tested in combat. You are what you are, and it better be enough.

I learned the art and practice of self-inventory from the grizzled old Vietnam veterans who surrounded me when I reported for duty at SEAL Team Two. I'd been a boy scout in my youth and understood the concept of being prepared, but the teams took this idea much more seriously, and for a good reason. Failure in combat was final, no do overs.

In business, unlike the military, the stakes are not nearly so dire. It may feel at times like they are, but they're not. However, the one thing that does exist for leaders in both realms of human endeavor is a deep sense of personal responsibility. Being on the hook to lead is often a lonely task, but also noble and vital in every organization.

In my experience, leading as a board member of a charity, leading a business division, and even leading middle school students on a field trip, all leadership is important but very few people are prepared for the challenges, leadership represents. If you are a leader or aspire to be one, this chapter will dial you into the first rule of leadership; understand both your capabilities and your limitations, then strive to eliminate those limitations. An honest self-assessment is critical if you want to survive, but even more important if you want to *thrive* as a leader.

Nature or Nurture?

Before we jump right into our self-awareness session, let's take a short journey to explore one of the oldest conflicts in leadership theory; are leaders born or created? Was Alexander the Great or General George Patton destined by fate to lead well, or were they simply blank slates, waiting for someone to teach them, train them, guide them, and finally develop them into successful leaders? It's a debate with a purpose.

Billions are spent every year in companies all over the country to groom managers and supervisors into effective leaders. If leaders cannot be educated into existence, if they can only be "discovered" and placed into key positions, then trying to sculpt regular people into the next Steve Jobs or Jeff Bezos is a waste of time and money, or is it?

My many years of being led and leading others, colors my point of view on this subject. I've concluded that there are natural behavioral traits and advantages associated with psychological resilience that play a major role in nurturing a person into a successful leader, and through mentoring turning a successful leader into a great leader. If these base characteristics are the only prerequisites to lead well, then I guess advocates of the nature theory have a strong case. But I'm not so sure.

Analysis of great leaders show a few common threads but nothing that is so definitive that indicates they were destined to lead, despite the post ascendancy rewrite of their personal story (Julius Caesar was a great leader and a great promoter of his own legend). Throughout human history, successful leaders have made a point to clean up their back story, remove the blemishes, and exaggerate the triumphs. This behavior is understandable, but it does modern leadership scholars a disservice when trying to understand the nature, nurture hypothesis.

More modern sources are accessible and therefore more

difficult to edit once a leader has become well-known. Teddy Roosevelt was a sickly young man, Harry Truman was a plain teenager without great promise... the list goes on.

A Leader in Crisis

The leader revealed by crisis is a common theme in mythology, popular literature, and our modern military history. This leader invariably, rises from obscurity like a phoenix, a young marine corporal saves his squad by leading a decisive charge, a dad miraculously lifts a heavy object off a child and directs the response that saves the child's life, a passerby sees mugging in progress and without regard for his own safety thwarts the attack and saves the victim.

We've all read stories like these and they're almost always true. Common people without leadership training or even aspirations to lead, become leaders, heroes, all in the blink of an eye. So, it must be something we're born with, right? A genetic capability that's present in select people, waiting for just the right opportunity to come forth, right? Not so fast.

This is where I come down on this age-old conflict in leadership theory. I believe human behaviors are shaped by their early childhood environment. By environment I mean to include all physical and psychological influences, good, bad, and worse, Influences that define a person's early character, sense of selfishness or selflessness. Influences that define a person's tolerance for person risk and failure. I've read over one hundred biographies of great leaders; all were flawed human beings in some form or fashion, but all were risk takers. All were willing to fail, sometimes fail many times, until they got it right.

Not all great leaders were saints. Morality and ethics are not historical prerequisites for successful leadership, just look at the long list of despots around the world and through history who led well and won, without concern for how they won. Today winning at any cost, by immoral or unethical acts, is unacceptable and illegal in most cases. In the United States and in most advanced nations around the world such behavior is legitimate grounds for a leader's removal and termination, if not jail time. Confused yet?

The nature vs. nurture debate hasn't been put to rest. Leadership is many things; it relies on a wide range of character traits and behaviors. It often doesn't reveal itself until crisis provides the opportunity to act. It rests on early influences and it can be developed. My personal experience is an example of this more complex formula. Strict parents, solid understanding of right and wrong. A period of continuous drama, upheaval, and relocation in my teens, then the crucible of SEAL training.

In my case, I also had an opportunity to watch great leaders and not so great leaders in the laboratory of life as well as in the military context. Then, when the time came, I found it in me to be a decisive leader. Not a perfect leader, or a great leader, but enough of a leader to see the potential, the possibilities. I firmly believe that most people, even you, can become successful leaders. I also fervently believe many of you can become *great* leaders!

Fear of Failure

If leadership in combat taught me anything it was perspective, especially as it relates to stress. More specifically, the fear of failure. When a spontaneous act of courage or leadership occurs without thought, without a plan, fear of failure is suspended. It's usually when we are alone in our thoughts with plenty of time on our hands, that the dragons of doubt prowl.

Every little consideration becomes an obstacle to success. Your boss, your partner, your co-worker, the industry, the weather, you get my point. Once you go down the trail of self-doubt it's hard to see the real world for what it is. Instead, you craft a world that's stacked the odds against your success, it is a fantasy, but a fantasy that will rob you of your desire to even try.

Failure is a part of life, all life. We are born, collect a lifetime of failures, and die. Some are astute enough to observe their failures objectively and learn. Others do not. History is full of examples where failing wasn't an impediment to final success. Failure is an opportunity to assess, to correct course, and to move forward, always forward. I was once an instrument rated private pilot. The training and testing are rigorous and when ready, a student must demonstrate to an FAA examiner, in the air, a series of take-offs, landings, complex maneuvers, and emergency procedures. They must also fly and approach busy airports using only the instruments located on the plane's console.

I retired with seven hundred and fifty-one free fall parachute jumps. The equivalent of civilian skydiving, advanced freefall operations taught aerodynamics, the same aerodynamics that applied to flying and controlling an airplane. I was comfortable in the cockpit and absorbed the instruction with relative ease. But when it was showtime, I choked. I failed both my private and my instrument rating flight tests. It hit me hard.

Months and months of preparation, even practice test flights with my flight instructor and yet when it was time to perform, I failed. I eventually passed the second time around and became a good pilot, but the humility of failing made me a better, more thoughtful pilot. The immediate aftermath of failure wasn't fun, but the lessons learned were invaluable. Embrace failure, it is your mentor.

Honest Self-Assessment

Nobody is perfect. Let me say that again. Nobody is perfect. Not the most famous business leader, most powerful and influential politician, not me, and not you. Perfection is a place we never visit, it's a stretch goal. It's the journey toward perfection, not the destination, that makes us stronger, better, wiser. We all change. Sometimes for the worse but more often for the better.

My secret technique, the one thing that has been the foundation of my leadership success, is the process of honest self-assessment. This appraisal method is the child of my many failures. I'm human. Once I experience the post screwup period of denial, I allow myself to reflect. I then scrutinize my failure repeatedly until I begin to see the truth. It happens unconsciously at first, but I soon gain clarity and insight, then I change what must be changed.

First, let me be clear. Self-scrutiny isn't enjoyable but it isn't meant to be a pity party either. The steps you take to list your personal and professional strengths and weaknesses will reveal reality, your reality. A reality you have the power to change. So, here's the key, humility. You must clear your mind of self-delusion and ego and be prepared to face the best and the worst in yourself. This isn't impossible, I do it routinely to become the best I can be.

I've found emphasizing the value of humility to be the most difficult attribute to coach or mentor in someone else. Most leaders improve a little, but few see the light and drop the mental constraint of an overwhelming ego. Revealing weakness is difficult for leaders, even more difficult for strong leaders who've discovered a way to compartmentalize their failings. They are comfortable projecting strength, even when inside they feel weak. Let me tell you, there's pure gold in remembering your mistakes and gleaning wisdom from them. The first step to enlightenment is to become humble!

A Position Specific Report Card

Sit down and pull out a piece of paper, or pull up a blank screen on your computer, and write or type the word Strengths. Then move down the page or screen a bit and type or write the word Weaknesses. You see where this is going. The key is honesty. And the key to honesty is humility. So, before you start this exercise clear your mind of ego, or social norms, or the last evaluation your boss gave you.

Clear your mind and act as if you were going to go to prison for perjury if you lie or embellish your answers. I'll share a trick, set a maximum number of listed weaknesses to ten. You must also match your ten faults with ten strong points. It's difficult to be all great or all messed up using that formula.

While listing more accolades and more issues may be more comprehensive, you want to choose the top ten in each category. If you can't hold yourself to ten go ahead and finish your longer lists. When finished, rank the opinions from one to ten starting with the best (strength) or worst (weakness) until you complete the list of ten opinions in each self-assessment category. Discard the extra work. Whichever path you take, you are left with twenty honest, humble, and actionable opinions about yourself. You're ready to move to the next step, study hall.

Position Specific Corrective Actions

I was kidding. You won't be required to go to an actual study hall, but you will be going to school. Our emphasis in this book is on moving the performance needle, making you a better or a more enlightened and successful leader. While I encourage you to perform the self-assessment regarding your overall capabilities and limitations in general, for now, just focus on the professional challenges.

It doesn't matter if you are already in a leadership position or aspire to fill one soon. The next step in this process will convert your weakness into virtue and your strength into an irresistible force of nature.

Every one of the twenty positive and not so positive issues you've identified must be explored and understood fully. Most of us dread acknowledging and writing down weaknesses in the first place. Researching those weaknesses however can be therapeutic. For example, several years ago one of the companies I led was considering a move into virtual training and education.

We were teaming up with a much larger defense firm and their people were throwing around terms and acronyms that baffled me and my team. We were strong in curriculum development and our learning experiences always received high marks from our customers. Now we felt like idiots. My team was becoming convinced we were the wrong company to partner with the big firm. What to do? I made a blanket statement to my team encouraging them to become more conversant in the language of virtual training and distance learning then went back to my desk and conducted a self-assessment, in this case regarding my technical knowledge and ability.

The recommendation several days after our initial meeting was to drop the initiative and move on. I calmly smiled and said no. Not only were we going to team with the large firm and produce what the government customer wanted, we were going to make our own proprietary virtual training product and use it as a proof of capability statement for marketing purposes. Why did I reject the consensus opinion of my team?

After making a list of my strengths and weaknesses I spent a week reading everything I could get my hands on regarding my professional shortfalls in the area of virtual training, or as I learned soon after beginning my quest, the world of instructional systems design or ISD. I read articles, watched webinars, read multiple industry related books through a forum of online cliff notes. While I worked and studied, my weaknesses became strengths, and my strengths gave me the confidence that we could accomplish what some of my people thought too difficult to try.

The contract was a success and so was our first ISD driven virtual training course. Believe in the power of change and commit to growing as a professional. It is the foundation of a successful business thinker and a critical prerequisite to become a creative leader!

Become a Student of Strategy

The prior example shows how you can use the self-inventory approach to self-awareness and improvement and apply it to a specific role or task. I suggest you take the method a step farther. You must think big, dream big, and prepare for big to become, well, big. The challenges you are aware of are a good place to start, but what about the one's you are not aware of? How about the challenges waiting for you just over the professional horizon?

There are many core skills and core areas of knowledge that form the bedrock of success in our life and in our work. The ability to speak well, the ability to write well, project planning, financial analysis, mentoring and coaching, the list goes on. These can be operational level targets for new learning and growth, or they can be new strategic categories for personal change and growth.

For example, the ability to speak well becomes the ability to do public speaking to large groups. The ability to write well becomes your first book on your industry or your insights. Maybe you don't see it yet but it's right there in front of you, the future needs a bigger you! Now is the time to start preparing!

Strategic self-assessment and operational level self-assessments should become a habit. You should practice the drill until it's a part of what you do, all the time. When confronted with difficulty in executing as a leader and when things appear to be, for the moment, smooth and easy. Many people ascend to a leadership position in their chosen field and once there, kick back and relax. They're the boss now. Everyone must answer to them, and no one should question their right to be the boss. Wonder, right? Except, life moves on. These days life moves on at an incredible speed. Resting on your throne and behaving as if you've "arrived" is a recipe for leadership disaster.

If you want to be chosen to lead, show you are a learning leader, a prepared leader, a humble leader. And while you scope out that new job, handle that next problem, save some time to think strategically, to think big. To do that you have to personally expand your competencies, increase your capabilities, and do this across the board. Reach higher, do this and I promise great opportunities will suddenly present themselves to you!

Winning is about Evolving

I don't want you to get the wrong impression. Being humble and being prepared won't eliminate risk or failure. What it will do is give you a constructive path to improvement. A fighter begins as a novice and as a novice makes more mistakes, suffering failure regularly. At the age of fifty-three I decided to get the equivalent of a black belt in Thai Boxing, the ancient art known as Muay Thai. I was a successful executive, financially secure, and oh yeah, a former Navy SEAL. What could possibly go wrong?

A lot can go wrong. My wife shuddered every time I came home from a session. The dark purple and green bruises all over my body made it clear to her I wasn't learning how to fight very well. She asked me to stop many times over the three years I trained, to take a break, perhaps pursue a less violent hobby. Of course, I didn't stop and eventually I got stronger, quicker, and smarter.

I trained with a former UFC strike coach who had over eighty professional kick boxing fights to his credit. He was six foot one with eight pack abs and a near eighty-inch reach. I was none of those things and it showed. It took me eighteen months to finally catch him with a jab to the chin for the first time, we were both surprised. It was to say the least, humbling yet enlightening at the same time.

Believe it or not, I applied my habitual self-assessment inventory process discussed in this chapter throughout my three-year struggle. Eventually, I did finish the program and my wife was there to cheer me on during my final test. While I failed, often miserably, every training day was a step forward. One training day at a time, I learned and grew wiser.

There was never going to be a day when I defeated my trainer. But every day I stepped out on the mat was a day I felt more capable of handling normal, non-professional fighters. Winning isn't always about getting a medal for being first, sometimes winning is simply evolving. If you think you're ready, if you know what you must do to evolve, then it's time for you to risk getting punched in the face.

Chapter Three

Mission Focus

"Teamwork is the ability to work together toward a common vision. The ability to direct individual accomplishments toward organizational objectives. It is the fuel that allows common people to attain uncommon results."
Andrew Carnegie

Dysfunctional leaders guiding great organizations or great leaders trying to drive dysfunctional organizations, take your pick. In either case, nothing much is accomplished. If you have conducted your self-inventory of strengths and weaknesses, and started working on upping your game, you are ready to evaluate your business. This may mean a small team, a department, a division, or an entire company.

This chapter will focus on measuring twice then cutting once. Evaluating the mission, redesigning the path to success, and aligning all resources in one cardinal direction.

What is the Mission?

Okay, this sounds insulting, but most leaders are thrown into the mix and as a result they never stop to figure out the strategic point of the exercise. Problem solving at the technical and operational management level can suck a leader into a deep chasm of details and facts, band aid fixes, and long desperate days. This isn't wrong, leaders must be ready to work hard, but before you jump in and start swinging you need to understand the reason the business exists in the first place.

Many companies do not have a well-crafted mission statement or if they do have one its long on style and short on actionable substance. Mission statements that read like advertising copy are useless to an organization and to the leaders trying to push everyone forward toward a common goal. A mission statement isn't a strategy. Think of it as a compass heading, a reference that is clear and unambiguous. For example, "We are all going to North Dakota for the next decade to establish a colony, grow corn, and sell it for a profit to the rest of the country" is an example of a straightforward mission statement.

The precise performance metrics expected at the end of that decade might be expressed in a strategy as tons of corn sold, total revenue from corn sales, or profit margin from corn sales. The operational leadership task is to chart the step by step path to execute the mission and attain the strategic goal or supporting goals. The simple mission statements are the easiest to understand and to follow. They also allow everyone to gauge threats and opportunities against a clear marker of success and intent.

If you do not have a coherent mission statement you need to create one, even if you are low level leader. Your team must have a cardinal direction and measurable performance goals. Once you understand the mission statement (or created one if it didn't exist), you are ready to study the status quo.

The Ant Farm

Many of the organizations I've worked in were chaotic. Crazy places to work with ineffective leaders and misaligned talent. People working long hours to achieve aims they didn't fully understand or appreciate. A cycle of task assigned, work, task completed, paycheck direct deposit, repeat. This happens in the military from time to time, even in special operations. Units are trained and equipped exceptionally well to do one thing, but then for expediency purposes, are used in an entirely different manner for a significant period, often long enough to distort operational focus and strategic coherency.

This disconnect between mission statement and use of these

elite units begins to twist and distort the entire organization. Supply chains of materials and people become incompetent. Soon, nobody coming up through the pipeline is trained for the new job and the gear they are issued doesn't work either.

Before the breaking point one of two things occurs. Either the unit is issued a new, appropriate mission statement that correctly lines up the processes, or the unit splinters off a new structure with the new mission focus. The original unit is directed back in line with the original mission and all is well.

I've seen much worse in the commercial marketplace. I use the term "Ant Farm" to illustrate the actual process and communications functions you often discover in an organization, a methodology inconsistent with the official chart with all the pretty boxes and lines. You know, the diagram you see in new employee or new leader orientation and then never see again, that one.

The Ant Farm is there, believe me. People and leaders in general are too focused on short term objectives to take the time to formally restructure their teams, groups, or companies to reflect how things are really getting done. The longer this goes on the worse the disconnect becomes. As a leader you need to take the time to observe, chart, and interview until you understand exactly what's happening. Then you need to create a new functional design that streamlines workflow and enhances clear communication.

Dry Powder

In the days when the military used primitive muzzle loaded weapons, having enough black powder, that wasn't spoiled by rain, was considered a measure of a person's readiness and ability to fight. As a leader, you should undertake efforts to determine what, if any resources, are available to you, sufficient to first execute, and second, improve operations. Resources include direct budget funding for your team or business, training materials, internal and external training programs, access to consultants, and availability of relevant technology. If you find you do not have any resources, it will be more difficult to realign the mission (if required) and redesign the organization. I was faced with this dilemma a few years ago.

A business division was in trouble with a major government customer. Official, written warnings from the government were received, and our prospects for keeping the contract didn't look good. I was hired to clean up the mess. I followed the advice given to you so far. I assessed my capabilities against the tasks and challenges in hand.

When I accepted the new leadership position I quickly plotted out a rigorous learning process and became a diligent student of the processes, systems, and assigned talent until I was up to speed on the unique aspects of my new assignment. I discovered right away that there wasn't a corporate, division, or departmental mission statement. Nothing. So, I created one, then issued it to my eight direct reports. So far so good! I then evaluated the workflow and contract requirements, redesigned the organization, and tweaked several key processes. Then I rolled up my sleeves and got to work.

Another key challenge I found was talent related. My people were not up to the task of executing at the level a full recovery required to return to standard (the prior performance standard). I knew returning to the prior status quo wasn't going to be enough. We were on the customer's performance and compliance watch list. A risk to be surveilled and perhaps mitigated. We needed to wow the customer, exceed expectations, and turn their frown upside down. But after my initial efforts to right the ship, my lofty expectations were not happening. I stepped back and reassessed the situation.

My people were a combination of high school graduates, ex-military, and a few college folks, few had business training or business experience. How did I miss that? My first impulse was to create an inhouse training program to improve their skills and knowledge. There were no resources available for that idea. So, out of necessity I decided to backstop the weak points by acting as the performance trainer for my team. It worked. Over the next three months we not only turned the contract around but also won rave reviews from the government customer. In this case I was the only dry powder available. Identify your available tools and assets and get to work fixing, repairing, and then improving. Then fight for more resources.

Mandate for Change

Another challenge I dealt with for years was trying to convince the person who'd just hired me to allow me to make the changes that were needed to execute and create a successful, well-functioning organization. I've concluded over time that positive change management requires a leader to learn how to influence the key decision makers and stakeholders in the hierarchy. The gate keepers, founders, boards, C-suite leaders, investors, lenders, they all get a vote. Often, they want dramatic upside results without shaking things up too much. In my experience, those are incompatible goals.

As the saying goes, you must break a few eggs to make an omelet. Now, I'm not saying it's okay to waltz in and just wreck the infrastructure. If you follow my guidance you will learn to understand your strengths and weaknesses as applied to your new job, you'll learn how things are being accomplished and you'll be able to match what is, against what *should be*. Of course, once you've completed this initial process you may find the status quo is satisfactory, you may want to change a few things, or worst case, you'll need to overhaul everything.

Before you do a word of caution. Don't light the fuse to blow things up until you've confirmed you have authority to make things better, no matter the solution. I mean a true mandate, backed by whoever you report to. A mandate with teeth supported with appropriate resources and people power. I used to live by the maxim "It's better to beg for forgiveness than ask for permission". That approach may work at a small level of play, but this theory can cause disaster in larger companies.

Emotions of Change

Everybody wants change for the better unless the change you contemplate implementing affects them. People are creatures of habit. They start confused, learn, become proficient, and then economically coast on that proficiency. They are an expert in their niche, and it feels good. They like the people they work with and they like the desk where they sit. They like the predictable work schedule, and they even like the room temperature just the way it is.

When you are preparing to pitch your master of change thesis to your boss consider basic human nature and the unintended consequences of your plan. The first reaction from most people upon hearing that change is in the wind is to ask themselves, *what will happen to me?* Be prepared to answer that question for them.

The second reaction to change is usually, *how can I keep things just the way they are?* Don't underestimate people's aversion to change or their willingness to slow your roll. Big or small, change is an emotional roller coaster for most people. Build in how you will address this aspect of your plan and be confident. Doing this will demonstrate you are thoughtful and empathetic. It will also show a seasoned boss that you are mature and capable of doing what you say you can do through people not despite them.

Workflow Alignment

Once you have approval, your mandate for change, it's time to go a little deeper than a redesigned organizational chart. During your analysis of the way things are you should have noted the flows that worked (preserve these processes) and the flows that did not work (eliminate or restructure these processes). Take time to diagram the internal supply chain of materials, support, communications, financial flows, critical information, and customer complaints.

Whatever key activities comprise the body of your delivered work. From start to finish. From idea to delivery. You need to frequently trace things back to your mission, your stated and desired strategic performance outcomes, to validate what you want to keep and want you must change. The mission and strategic performance metrics are your friend. Stay in touch with these, carry them around in your pocket. Do not allow yourself to stray after coming this far.

Here's the tough part. You'll need to drop down one more level of organizational design and design the actual jobs, the functions and positions that will allow your new machine to purr like a finely tuned race car. Be precise, especially with brand new positions. Modify existing positions as required by formally amending the position descriptions. I know this is a lot of work, but it will pay off, trust me!

Maybe you were promoted from within and personally know all the people who will be affected by your master plan, or maybe you came in from somewhere else, in either case here are a few job design tips to prevent you from making the same mistakes I've made over the years.

Position Design Tips

Here's the first tip. Don't put a name next to a position. That's right. Do not place the name "Veronica" the level II accountant next to the new position labeled "Financial Business Analyst". Here's the reason. Your job design approach must be pure of heart and mind. The mission and strategic objectives must be supported by the new organizational design, and the new organizational design must be aligned to perform in slightly or entirely new ways. Think functional elements of execution not specific people. This will result in a clean structure from the bottom all the way up to the top.

So far so good. But what happens if you decide to design the position around the existing talent? When you personalize the jobs to conform to the people currently in place? I'll tell you what happens, a train wreck. A compromise in design that will haunt you if it is allowed to exist. Stay true to the redesign method as described, you'll reap the benefits as you begin to exercise your new platform, trust me.

Tip number two, don't assume the subordinate leaders, managers, and supervisors you have in place now are going to be able to handle your new normal. Leave these new positions blank as well. Contorting well-thought out designs to keep a management personality in place is a recipe for dysfunction and its dysfunction you're trying to avoid. Many leaders have the same resistance to change as any other employee, they are human after all. Expect to be vigorously lobbied by some to maintain the status quo and others for a promotion or even better titles. Did I mention human nature is in play here?

Tip number three, if you are involving employees and leaders in crafting the new normal be attentive to attitudes revealed while outlining or brainstorming the change you are contemplating. Note who is honestly excited, they are either fans or working hard to appear they are fans. Note who is paying lip service to change, they are not impressed or convinced. And finally, note those who become strangely quiet and introspective. These folks may be considering an emergency departure before things get too "crazy".

Soak it all in and use your observations to do a little personal lobbying, lead one employee and manager at a time. Your firmly conveyed proposals and patient leadership can go a long way to converting and convincing people that change can be good thing. Improvement that is reasonable and achievable *if you all pull together*. You may lose a few, that's okay, it's time to see who's ready to step up their game, anyway.

The Pace of Organizational Change

You don't have to look hard to find books on organizational change management. Most on the market speak to the reader using business school language and academic citations to prove their points. I've spent years reading these and other business books and I've learned from them, but I've also come to a few conclusions based solely on my personal business experience.

First, there aren't many books written for the small business owner or for the leaders in mid-sized businesses. The classic narratives are long on large scale organizational architecture and supporting systems, and short on executable ideas and insights. Business textbooks tend to recant business history and case studies but stop short of speaking to what most leaders are looking for, traction in the trenches. One exception to this is the author, Malcolm Gladwell. His books are on my shelf because they speak to the physics and context of business. His insights are universally applicable and reflect observations, not abstract theory or wishful thinking.

A corrective program of real change takes thought, planning, and tender nurturing. You should be prepared for a lengthy process. The study and observation period itself may take months. The redesign work in my experience, is often accomplished on weekends and nights, after you finish your daily leadership chores. Pace yourself, be determined to complete the steps outlined in this chapter and you will succeed in creating a plan that is sound, a plan that addresses the rational eighty-five percent of the critical elements that you've identified that require adjustment. I know you can accomplish great things, be patient but resolute. It will happen, I promise!

This is a big topic, and I could write a separate book focused only on organizational change. My intent here is to expose you to the art and motivate you to learn more. For the most part I've learned how to analyze organizational dysfunction through mentoring and good old on the job training. I've grown departments into divisions, and divisions into standalone companies. I done this, for the most part with scarce resources. That's not my preference, but I know it can be accomplished. Don't let a lack of resources be justification to accept the status quo.

I've been able to convince Navy Admirals to follow one design for change and then was shot down by the same Admirals on other projects. The same holds true in my twenty-four years in commercial business. Sometimes I win, sometimes I lose, but I always try. I try to communicate, influence, pitch, sell, and beg for approval and for resources to execute. You can do this too. Try it and you'll see. Big change requires big dreams, a big heart, and a tolerance for big risks. Are you ready?

SEAL Mission Focus

The stereotype of military practitioners mindlessly focused on a mission, do, or die, is appropriate in desperate times but hardly the rule. Special operators are always trained and drilled in nimble thinking. They apply this mindset before, during, and after a mission. Nimble thought goes into forging a well-crafted, multi-phase operation and mission execution is a series of mini steps and small judgements. Each is an opportunity to think creatively. Afterward, lessons learned are bandied about and notes taken to improve performance on the next operation. This is referred to as a hot wash process.

In the late 1990s the SEAL community recognized their young officers were applying the tactics of hostage rescue to all tactical scenarios. In a hostage rescue mission, there is an imperative implied by the limited time available to resolve the threat and save the hostages. Appearing suddenly, sliding down ropes, kicking in doors, blowing holes in cinder block to gain access, and racing into a structure or vessel to save the hostages is the standard methodology. It is a far cry from the green painted ninja SEALs of Vietnam fame. Sneaking and peeking, extraordinarily successful, and rarely getting caught let alone detected. In the last decade of the Twentieth Century this mental and tactical shift over time was a serious issue.

Young men are easy to fire up but hard to calm down. The various SEAL mission categories required stealth, cool minds, and creative techniques to succeed. There are plenty of military units designed to attack and swarm an objective, SEALs don't do that as a rule, and shouldn't automatically introduce a violent resolution as the be all, end all method of executing on target. Yet it happened. Slowly, the DNA of the once clever warriors who fought in Vietnam was replaced with a new, aggressive mode of thinking.

The answer was to reevaluate the training pipeline to find where this all in, aggressive attitude was being taught, and if necessary, go back even as far as the recruiting messaging to see if we were attracting men predisposed to fighting aggressively rather than intelligently. The result was a community wide recognition that the training cadre on average had become less experienced. There were few or no Vietnam era warriors left to weigh in on mission mindset. This became a focus of retraining the instructors, reviewing, and correcting curriculum, and changing performance training exercises to allow for intelligent judgement. The do or die scenarios were scripted to reflect a balanced and thoughtful approach to winning.

Mission focus sounds good, aggressive, even powerful. It's tossed around frequently by former military consultants to business and glorified as a be all, end all solution to execution and performance. I'm here to tell you this is a shallow interpretation at best. It is easy to get jacked up and charge into the fray without truly studying the situation at hand. Nimble leadership requires such intellectual consideration, *before* you launch everybody enthusiastically into the battle. Stay clever, stay tuned into situational reality. Maintain an open mind to executing your mission and do so in thoughtful steps. This isn't about dragging your feet, this is about not rushing ahead and dropping into the tiger pit. Focus intelligently.

Chapter Four

The Talent Show

"Great vision without great people is irrelevant."
Jim Collins, Good to Great

For me, creating a new organizational structure, one that in part or in whole, aligns properly and coherently with the new normal, is a cathartic management exercise. I know from hard experience that a dysfunctional structure will cause mind-numbing challenges to leadership, at every level, every day.

These structural challenges are self-inflicted wounds that can and must be rectified. Once the new jobs are created on paper, the leader has one more task to complete before taking his or her new structure out for a test drive: an honest and professional evaluation of the talent pool.

This leadership responsibility is often emotional and so unpleasant that many great restructures die a slow death, never being implemented. Conflict avoidance and a sincere desire to retain all your leaders and employees, will weigh you down with guilt, remorse, or even dread. Yet, if restructuring is truly needed, what is your alternative? I suggest the price of side stepping this responsibility is the possible demise of your company, not by competitors, but due to your unwillingness to grit your teeth and lead the charge.

Leaders must seek to understand the strengths and weaknesses of their people before matching them to the newly designed jobs in the revitalized company structure. You must seek to understand everyone's capabilities and limitations. Once this honest appraisal is completed, it's time for you to get to work, upgrading skills and knowledge where necessary. You can do this successfully by applying honesty, intellectual integrity, inspiration, mentorship, revamped training programs, and by applying empathy to achieve results.

Business is a funny thing. Scaling up or down, a leader is faced with clear moments when decisions must be made. Is Bob able to learn the new normal in the time required? Can Susan do several tasks or is she only capable of linear task management? Does Steve have what it takes to work without supervision as the leader of his new team? Multiple teams? To a leader these moments feel emotional, not intellectual. They represent a personal crisis because honesty is clarity, clarity demands action, and action has consequences.

The emotional delay is illogical, but it's normal behavior for all leaders. Doing what is best for the organization going forward often means people will lose their jobs. I'm not speaking of the Peter Principle, the theory that people tend to rise to the level of their own incompetence. This isn't a corporate upward mobility problem. This is a dilemma usually brought on by rapid business success that drives parabolic increases in almost every business activity, challenging the status quo.

Leadership is Human Resources Management

So, you have created the new department, division, or company on paper. You've designed new positions, and redesigned existing ones to new standards. It's time to take the next step. Should you hand over this part of the process to the person or department trained and paid to assess the existing talent and hire the new blood? Isn't this what human resources is for?

In my opinion, leaders frequently make this mistake. Change, especially on a large scale, is a leadership job, not a human resources job. While this might make sense to you from an emotional self-preservation point of view, letting human resources lead the charge will often cause more harm than good.

Remember, this is your plan of action, your corrective measure, your change to lead. Delegating the talent portion to subordinate leaders or the human resources department will create a gap between your stated vision for change, and the way others end up executing their delegated tasks. Stay engaged. Stay focused on the end state, the purpose that incited you to reorganize. Do not delegate the tough calls, the evaluation of existing employees, or the selection of the new talent. Give your new plan a chance to be born, survive, and succeed by making sure these critical elements are executed under your watchful eye.

Don't Bend Design to Fit Talent

So, you are going to shepherd this thing through to a successful conclusion. I have been in this position as both a subordinate leader and as a CEO, and it sucks. You start small, with a narrow band of products or services and a small pool of customers. If you are successful, the customer pool grows, and as it grows you must decide how to cope with the strain on the existing organization. For most small and medium-sized businesses this simply means adding more of what you have.

For example, one salesperson becomes two, then four. If you make a product the effect of growth means hiring more designers, developers, assemblers. This works for a while until you reach your first tipping point, the moment when it suddenly occurs to you that doubling down on the current structural design, and talent to task alignment, will no longer fix the growth challenges or it's wildly inefficient and expensive.

Proactive Scaling

In 2006, I was a senior executive in a rapidly growing company. We were growing in every possible category, services, products, customers, worldwide geographic reach, and making a lot of money while doing it. The wheels started to come off the wagon around year three of this rapid expansion. Hiring twenty more bookkeepers wasn't going to work. Hiring an army of low level logistics technicians wasn't working either.

Many of the company's senior leaders had never operated a complex multi-million-dollar business before. While some had led military organizations the two worlds were vastly different in practice. These leaders did not hire key subordinate management layers as we grew. Management specialists who could help create an efficient and professional department or division. This shortfall ultimately resulted in a hollow organization.

We had a few dynamic and insightful bosses at the top trying to personally motivate, evaluate, and direct thousands of technical level employees. Lacking specialist management personnel in finance, marketing, transportation, and business operations, left us blind to what was coming, a functional train wreck. Everyone was willing to work hard, and few ever took time off, but effort and heart just wasn't sufficient to correct the mess.

I wish I could say I was the only leader with the experience and vision to see what had to be done but that wasn't the case. We were going from $200 million a year in revenue to $1 billion a year and we were leveraging resources, business systems technology, and human capital, better suited for a company making $30 million a year. I walked into the President's office one day after some soul searching and told him what I thought was happening and what I thought we should do.

What I suggested was to recreate the company on paper, a new, more robust, and capable organization. I told him to visualize the building as a container full of talented people. Then suggested we dump the container of people onto the parking lot and begin a reassessment of every single person.

The point of this metaphor was to show him how to reevaluate and reassign most of our employees. They were great people, and we should retain as many as possible. By applying the new business structure and its new position descriptions and qualifications, as a litmus test. Determining logically and appropriately, who we would retain and who would move on.

This process would also reveal all the gaps in talent assignment lining up a drive to hire new blood.

The President thought about my idea for a few weeks then relieved me of my duties as head of a $128 million dollar a year business division. He then sequestered me away from day to day management tasks and asked me to execute my idea. Reform the company into a new, more appropriate structure. He directed me to identify systems shortfalls and create new position descriptions. Then he told me to "do that box dump thing" onto the parking lot and start the process of smart personnel reassignment.

It took time to rework a company that was growing exponentially every day, but we were able to complete the restructuring and eighty percent of the employees were retained and reassigned to operate in the new normal. It wasn't perfect. Many employees were retained by their leaders in the hope they would learn to cope or keep up with the pace and complexity, regretfully, most did not.

Over six months, we added more mid-level management talent, a new layer of technical supervisors in every category of business execution and focused particularly hard on upgrading our finance and accounting capabilities. Throughout all this change management I was the architect but not the engineer. Hundreds of people solved the problems and suffered through the laying off of their people, many of whom were friends or longtime associates. Once completed, the company was able to continue growing in a more stable manner.

Treat Departing Talent with Respect

Even if your passionate desire to evolve feels like an emergency, I suggest you look at each employee individually. Look at their abilities (the things you rely on them for each day) and their capabilities (the additional things they could do for the company). If you are scaling down labor costs due to tough times or reducing labor due to automation, your employees will be expecting bad news.

Try to give everyone as much official notice of the changes that are coming as feasible and ensure all leaders, not just your human resources team, are fully aware of the plan, the schedule, and the general truth of things. They need to know why you are changing the status quo. This is not only professional it also takes away the fear of the unknown and aligns change with optimism instead of fear.

While it doesn't eliminate the possibility of losing a job, if done right and quickly, your employees will understand, adjust, and seek employment elsewhere if they choose to. Far too many businesses keep this change management secret and then surprise the affected employees with their fate. This is always counterproductive.

New Blood

So, to repeat, be true to the plan. The new or amended organization relies on your well-crafted job designs and those rely on your resolve to fill the positions with truly capable and qualified professionals. This process should begin as soon as possible after you finish creating the new positions so that your skill inventory of existing employees and management leadership is near completion when you are in the last phases of making a job offer to new hires.

This parallel approach will pay dividends. Reviewing resumes and holding initial interviews will give you a better sense of what the talent market looks like. It allows you to evaluate the potential new hire against the existing employee talent pool to see if your internal appraisals are fair. This parallel method also compresses the timeline for change, reduces the transition turmoil, and allows you to draw in fresh thinking and insights through the interview process.

The objective here is to minimize operational disruption as

you shift gears from the old way of conducting business to the new way of doing things. Set the new hire dates to coordinate with any employees departing the company, preferably using exit bonuses or severance packages to make the change as smooth as can be expected.

Design, Function, and Fit

As noted earlier, we are not talking about a wholesale replacement strategy. We are looking at the strengths and weaknesses of each existing employee against the new position design and the new objectives. Several years ago, I had a direct report responsible for managing millions of dollars in trade show activities all around the United States. He was exceptional at communicating with logistics and event management people *outside our company*.

At the trade shows, he was a wizard, dazzling potential customers with relevant product facts and specifications, but at home, in the company environment, this magnificently autonomous personality who was so single-mindedly able to shine on the road, was a hot mess, causing widespread discontent. Eighty-five percent of this person's position requirements were more than met but the turmoil created by the substandard fifteen percent was a big problem.

I did not want to lose him. So, after much thought, I simply made him a remote worker. This was a time almost fifteen years ago when working from home wasn't looked upon favorably by senior management in our country. My decision reduced the cultural pain and the eliminated complaints generated by his infrequent but damaging appearances in our corporate offices. I received considerable criticism from my peers for doing this but oddly, the very people who could not stand to work with this person were demanding he be forced to come into the office.

I reported to a President who understood my logic but even he questioned the idea after others lobbied against my decision.

Thankfully, today we are all much more comfortable with remote or virtual work designs. The point is this, your task is to make sure the person fits the new position as designed. Before taking the easy road, remove and replace, think all the options through carefully, employee by employee. There might be a better way to assist them in becoming the contributor you're looking for.

Culture Counts

Hiring the right person or designing a position and filling it with an existing employee feels straightforward, more science than art, but in my experience, this is rarely the case. Resumes for existing (or new candidates) are written to address the position description. In the case of existing employees with a long tenure, the resumes on file no longer reflect their full value, if they ever did and they certainly don't reflect what their workload and scope has evolved into overtime. Why would a candidate put "horse whisperer" or "magazine editor" on a resume crafted to land a job as a Logistics supervisor?

You see the problem. We get what we ask for, a monotone response to a monotone request. It's the process we use for normal day to day human resources recruiting but interestingly enough, not the process used by top executive headhunters. For example, professional headhunters have candidates fill out extensive questionnaires, take competency and compatibility tests, and interview by phone and in-person several times. Each interview aiming to uncover a different facet of the candidate's personality, professional methods, leadership philosophy, you get the picture. This more exhaustive approach tends to be successful. Why don't we use it for all hiring?

The Rocky Road to Execution

The old maxim that first impressions are lasting impressions is true when it comes to recruiting and hiring talent. It is also true when you are repurposing existing employees to align with the new way forward. Many organizations see the recruiting and hiring process as a unilateral decision, they are in the driver's seat and it is their opinion and judgment that matters, the candidate's impression of you isn't an important part of the hiring equation.

This point of view is both shortsighted and harmful to your plan to improve performance. Your best opportunity to wow a candidate with your company's revitalized vision for the future is when you are interviewing them. It is also vitally important to sell this vision to the employees and leaders you will retain.

Treat these retained employees the way you would if wooing a prospective strategic candidate. Give them the pitch, the positive energy, and then answer all their questions. Remember, they are suffering a thousand deaths every night, tossing, and turning and wondering if the changes that are coming will be harmful to them personally and professionally. Act as if they have a choice too because they do. They are critical to your success as any new hire.

Inspire the new candidates. Many of them will not pass the scrutiny of your hiring process but they will repeat what they experienced. In a niche market, a narrow professional category, or in a community situated around your business or industry, there are a multitude of influencers, current customers and potential customers, and competitors. The vision you impart during this selection phase will be repeated outside the confines of the company environment.

People will take notice and often, exceptional talent will head toward the bright light your company represents. Customers will become more loyal, and new prospects will either seek out your services and products or be more open to your sales presentations. Inspiration and vision are unfortunately rare in my experience, but they are a powerful one, two punch. Apply them and watch the magic unfold!

Time to Pick up Speed

Okay, strap yourself in and hold on tight. This is when the real fun begins. I coached youth football for a few years and was amazed at how rewarding it felt. I recognized at the time, a few years after leaving the Navy, that coaching kids through a season of football was much like the process of taking a new SEAL platoon and forging them into a well-oiled machine. In a sixteen-man SEAL platoon, there were multiple categories of administrative responsibility. Diving operations, weapons and demolitions, parachute operations, intelligence, engineering, and so on.

One enlisted SEAL was assigned to each critical task or area of responsibility. However, everyone in the SEAL platoon also had secondary areas of responsibility. We built redundancy and bench strength by having many people cross qualified. A typical SEAL might be the primary expert on parachute operations but also an understudy learning to become the lead expert in dive operations. This approach, I found, was transferrable to the football field. Youth football was never going to be the same

My coaching time was fun, but it was also enlightening. Aside from the obvious physical training correlation with my SEAL history, I found that building core expertise at each football position wasn't enough. I needed to build redundant strength and do so starting from the first practice of the season. The kids were oblivious to my master plan, but the parents weren't. They complained I was confusing their children by teaching them too many positions. These players were ten years old and I knew the DNA hadn't kicked in yet. Who knew what little George would look like in a few years? Would he be small? Tall and skinny? Or large and in charge?

I trained my players with an eye to the future. They would all know how to play the game at multiple positions making transition easier when that DNA did kick into gear. My son was held back his freshman year of football to play recreational football. He was five foot six and one hundred and twenty-five pounds soaking wet. By the end of his first year of high school, he was over six feet tall and weighed over one hundred and sixty pounds. DNA changes opportunities in the sport of football. This philosophy of cross training and building bench strength for the future paid dividends in football and in later years. I applied it to business, and lo and behold, it worked wonderfully.

We have come a long way. Your initial mission and organizational analysis resulted in a need to restructure. Your restructure required new position design and redesign of existing ones. You had to reevaluate your existing population of employees and recruit new blood. Congratulations, you are halfway there! Now it's time for you to forge and flex your new organization, your new team. It's time to lead through the confusion toward excellence. Here we go!

Chapter Five

Training, Coaching, and Mentoring

"Leadership is lifting a person's vision to high sights, the raising of a person's performance to a higher standard, the building of a personality beyond its normal limitations."
Peter F. Drucker

Once you are centered, openminded, and receptive to new information and new ideas; and once you have gauged the abilities of your team, it is time to create a business with a bias for action, high energy, and disruptive thinking. In the role of coach, you will use every tool and technique available to nudge each player in the team toward personal and professional improvement, with an emphasis on a clear vision of the team's mission and purpose.

Navy SEAL Teams assign trainers, coaches, and mentors, to provide the members of that military unit with knowledge-based learning, critical skills development, and when ready, enlightened empowerment. Many corporations also do this to good effect. My take on each of these three methods of improvement is straight forward. When building or rebuilding a business, holistically or in part, you need to be ready to invest time and energy into improving the performance of every person and then be willing to drive collective team efforts to a higher level of play.

My experience has been that leaders understand the value of training, coaching, and mentoring but fall short of implementing one, two, or all three of these methods. The common rationalizations I hear are lack of money, too little time, or too few qualified people to manage and deliver each of these methods while simultaneously running day to day operations.

I must admit, you must be comfortable investing scarce resources today to ensure improvements in creative and productive human behavior in the future. This level of comfort and forward thinking is rare in smaller companies. New employees or members are expected to show up ready and stay that way. This hope-based approach feels rugged and tough minded but it's shortsighted as well as dead wrong. Unless your business is static, or worse, declining, your employees need to keep pace with the increased volume, increased complexity, increased velocity, or a combination of these factors. They need to be developed.

Training to a Technical Standard

My definition of training helps me to separate it from the concepts, focus and expected outcomes of coaching and mentoring. Training is often used as a catch-all term encompassing any effort to deliver new information or skills, at any level, and for any length of time, to employees and members of companies. Training, in my opinion, has specifically defined elements delivered to a tightly defined standard, in a specific period.

The first way training is different from coaching and mentoring is the focus on specific learning tasks or elements that collectively add up to the addition of a new skill or imparting new understanding. Technical training is used for all types of specialties, physicians, carpenters, truck drivers, military personnel, all benefit from initial credentialling training and follow on learning. The term technical in this case means itemized, specific, and directive. You must turn the valve to the right, you must throttle the airspeed back, you must perform the function in this order. You get the picture.

Before I went to SEAL training, I was trained to be a RADAR operator and Air Traffic Controller by the Navy and graduated with all the skills necessary to operate the mechanical equipment found on a sophisticated Navy ship. After many weeks of intense schooling, I passed all my proficiency exams and practical exercises. I was ready to go to a ship and begin my assignment. Even though I was a proud graduate of an intense training program I assure you no Captain of a United States ship of war would have relied on my abilities without a team of coaches putting me through drills and observing, correcting, admonishing, and praising my efforts. Advanced training wasn't enough, it was the beginning.

In the SEALs, I attended over twenty schools and courses of all kinds. In each of these courses, I was taught specific procedures and techniques to perform a specific role. When these courses were over, I was ready to assume the role of a qualified participant, but I wasn't considered an expert, not yet. Experience, coaching, and insightful mentoring were needed before I was considered an expert.

The second way I differentiate training is the application of well-defined standards. Training information presented without a standard of performance is hollow and ineffective. If you were a surgeon would it matter if you removed all the tumor or would a part of the tumor be sufficient? Should ground maintenance inflate all the aircraft tires to the standard air pressure or are two out of four tires good enough?

Leaders who create or review training curriculum, or monitor and observe training, should make sure the standards of performance for everything being taught are a part of the material delivery method and the final student testing. Training without standards is like spitting into a strong wind, an embarrassing outcome.

The third-way training differs from its two cousins, coaching and mentoring, is duration. Training is classically designed to the length of time it takes to deliver the information, practice the skill or skills, and test or validate that the student has attained the course objectives through personal demonstration. This means training can be as short as an hour in length, and as long as eight years in duration. Training can be held as required, scheduled or can be impromptu. It can be part of onboarding new hires, or as part of formal training pipelines for professionals in trade schools, colleges, and universities.

Coaching to an Operational Standard

When does training end and coaching begin? It depends on the definitions you chose to use. I think coaching is a long-term effort to improve the performance of someone who is already trained to do what they are supposed to do. Coaching is an intimate, one on one engagement. Training can be conducted this way but is more often executed in large groups for efficiency sake.

Coaching is an operational area of behavioral influence. You can teach culture, but it takes coaching to ingrain a culture in every individual. You can train a group as a team, but it takes coaching to move the team from aspirational goals to execution and excellence. Coaching is leading behavior through surveillance and modification.

Coaching also takes wisdom, sound judgment, and an understanding of human nature. Of course, you need a certain level of technical knowledge, but good coaches are not always technical experts. To train a person or a group requires a high level of technical expertise and specific functional knowledge. Wisdom or judgment is optional.

Both approaches to human behavior and performance improvement require solid communication skills but coaching also requires the ability to listen and understand. A proficient coach also communicates to motivate and guide. Training instructors would like you to be motivated to learn the material or the skill being taught, but they are not obligated to *move* you to do so.

Most training tends to be one-way information flow, instructor to student. Most coaching is an interactive, two-way dialogue. Both delivery methods are important with training usually preceding coaching in the developmental process. So, now that your people are trained and working successfully toward their, and the company's professional objectives. What comes next?

Mentoring to Achieve Peak Excellence

The terms coaching and mentoring have blurred in recent years with the advent of executive coaching, leadership coaching, and peak performance coaching focused on senior management in midsize to large companies and corporations. Most often in practice, these engagements, internally resourced or outsourced to consultants, are really mentorships.

An internal or external mentor can be assigned to you by your boss, a board of directors, or you can seek out and retain a mentor on your own. Mentors come in all sizes and shapes and every industry, profit or non-profit, benefits from the use of mentoring programs. Mentors are highly focused on one individual's success. They may be paid to do so or if you're lucky, they agree to do so as a favor. In any case, having a mentor can help you through unique professional challenges.

I have been privileged to have several mentors in my professional progression from enlisted SEAL to officer, while a portfolio manager, and in my current role as CEO and Chief Strategy Officer. My mentors seem to have appeared at just the right time for me to bridge my abilities from a place where training and coaching had reached the limits of their helpfulness.

As a SEAL you always prepare for war or at least conflict at some scale. Short, chaotic surges of uncertainty and high risk followed by boredom and continuous effort to maintain critical technical skills. My first significant mentor came early in my first five years as a SEAL. Bob Gallagher's nickname was "the Eagle" and he was a veteran of countless combat missions in Vietnam. Bob was highly decorated, a recipient of the Navy Cross, the second-highest honor presented for valor next to the Congressional Medal of Honor. We all looked up to this incredible warrior.

The Eagle was a quiet unassuming man who was so soft-spoken he seemed to whisper his orders. After two years in the SEAL teams, I was assigned to the training department, reporting to this legend. The eagle was straight forward, clear-minded, and brief, very brief. He didn't give speeches and he didn't berate us when unsatisfied with our work. You just knew you'd failed to meet his exacting standards.

There was over a decade difference in age between us but that didn't matter. I asked thousands of questions, about war, combat, decisions under fire, tactics, training, anything that might make me smarter, give me an edge. I hungered for this level of wisdom because you see I had transcended training and being coached. Now I was the coach, helping others as a primary duty assignment in the SEAL Team Two training department.

The Eagle was my secret weapon. If only I could learn half of what he knew I would be far ahead of my peers and more than ready for the day I saw combat. I didn't see combat for another ten years and when I did, I was a commissioned officer leading SEALs. I'd almost forgotten all I'd learned from the Eagle ten years earlier, that is until combat became real for me.

The Eagle's maxims, admonishments, insights, sneaky tricks, and simple tactics flooded into my brain along with the adrenaline rush and the fear of failure. I immediately realized the value of his sage advice and mentoring and as a result, I cast aside much of the new, over thought and overly complex doctrine of special operations taught in the SEAL teams and instead embraced the Eagle's common sense game plan for success in combat and it worked!

Years later, when I began my new life out of uniform, I found that the job of financial advisor and portfolio manager required more than brains and knowledge of the stock market, it required clients! I began that second career without a single client account and none on the horizon. My undergraduate degree in business administration and my graduate degree in management were comprehensive and enlightening but they fell short in one critical area required for business success, how to sell.

Don't get me wrong, those B-school professors spoke about sales, I knew "sales" was important and why. They just didn't teach us *how* to sell anything. I realized I had to learn to sell and learn fast or my new career would be over before it began. The financial services firm's sales guidance was pretty much confined to a hardy good luck!

Of course, my firm had sales expectations, the compensation was all based on sales commissions, no salary. I was expected to generate sales input by finding prospects, pitching my services to them until they capitulated and opened an account. Then I needed to create an investment plan and start buying investments to support that plan. When that was done the sales commission system would spit out my share of that sale. Neat and simple.

I had a family member, Matt Fitzpatrick, a high school graduate and navy veteran of four years (electronics), who was making over two hundred and fifty thousand dollars a year selling meat wrapping machinery to grocery stores. In desperation (on day four after passing my certifications to invest other people's money) I called him up and explained my problem. At that point, every cell in my body was screaming I should quit and find another profession. It felt logical to quit. I wanted to blame my professors for screwing up my education and my firm for "setting me up" to fail miserably.

Matt's soothing voice on the other end of the line began to talk me down off the ledge. He started by inventorying my personal and professional skill sets, one strong point at a time. After thirty minutes of this question and answer session, he paused. At this point, I fully expected him to agree with my bleak assessment and suggest I quit, find a good salaried job, and move on, but that's not what happened.

Matt became my mentor. His first observation, based on his thorough skills assessment, was that I should forget cold calling and other direct sales techniques and instead, grow my business using informative seminars. He explained how my briefing and teaching experience in the Navy dovetailed perfectly with the skills required to stand in front of a group of potential clients looking for help. I took his sage advice and went on to perfect the art of investment and financial planning seminars, often holding two a week in the first two years of my new profession. My business ramped up rapidly.

These days, I find I'm spending much of my time evaluating companies to purchase or assessing the market value of the companies in our portfolio of businesses. This process is a skill and an art I did not develop on my own, you guessed it, I had a powerful mentor who showed me the way. His name is Bill Hayes.

Mentoring is useful in helping your best people push past their self-imposed limits and it can assist your leaders to evolve as they struggle to cope with greater levels of risk and responsibility. If you don't have a mentor, it's never too late. Also suggest or impose the use of mentorships for your subordinate leaders. Make sure you apply this effective method of performance or behavior modification; it will pay big dividends for you. It did for me!

The Top to Bottom Talent Mix

So, now we've reviewed three effective ways to improve the capabilities, skills, and knowledge of your employees and leaders. It's important to note that training, coaching, and mentoring are not equally impactful for every level of your organization. You will need to create a plan that provides what each level needs and make sure your leaders are following the plan.

I enjoy all three methods of directed learning. I've always loved to teach, and coaching was a skillset practiced in the Navy and soon after leaving the service. Mentoring was a learned skill later in life. Mentoring can quickly spiral into therapy and that's a pitfall of engaging in mentoring before learning how to do it effectively. This goes for being mentored also. Don't approach your mentor with the weight of the world and unload it all on them. Stay focused on what they can do to assist you, professionally. Leave out the office gossip, the turf battles and internal office politics. Stay pure to learning how to perform better and it will be rewarding for you and for your mentor.

In my experience, most leaders appreciate the attention I give them as a coach or mentor, but they do not always pay that level of personal and professional attention forward to their direct reports. Don't assume your company-wide program is on autopilot. You will have to monitor, measure, and provide your leaders with an example to emulate. If you do, you will reap the rewards, I promise you!

Ramping up Expectations

While you are training, coaching, and mentoring don't forget to begin ramping up expectations. You're building a dynamic, strong, and highly capable organization that will need to hear from you why they are going through all this trouble. Sprinkle around your dreams and aspirations for the business, as a regular mantra.

Don't be afraid to show a little emotion, to show passion, it is the currency of motivation and where words and plans fail, intensity of commitment sells. Be aspirational but add details, goals as concepts, target dates for expected growth, and then tie all that to the promise of rewards for all who help you reach those targets. Stay upbeat and be ready for the change/fear cycle to spin up again.

Change and growth represent a risk to many people, explain why that doesn't have to be the case. Lay out a case for making a difference too, in your industry, your community, in the lives of your customers or external stakeholders. People need to know they are being impactful in a positive way. Encourage employees to brainstorm ideas and they will surprise you.

Preparing for New Performance Requirements

As you push your people to greater professional heights you should be working with your leaders and your human resources team to craft specific compensation programs that properly incentivize top leaders, middle management, technical experts, project leads, and anyone else who will make a difference.

As the CEO of an employee-owned group of companies, I have the foundation of shareholder-employees to leverage. This isn't always an incentive as most people have a difficult time associating long hours and working weekends with an increase in share value in the future. I suggest you use a mix of event or project-based incentives that help your people stay motivated to win, for themselves and the company.

You are now ready to push the throttle forward. I'm aware that while you've been reorganizing operational structures, adjusting processes, fine tuning systems, evaluating talent, hiring new blood, and increasing the internal development effort to get the new normal up to battle speed, that you've also been dealing with regular business demands. This is the challenge.

Most leaders start with good intentions, but work gets in the way. To adopt the tenets of this book and achieve extraordinary outcomes, you will have to burn the candle at both ends and so will many of your people. As the chief architect, you are also obligated to be the head cheerleader, therapist, focused trainer, a motivated coach, and a wise mentor. You can do this, but you need to factor in the stress change brings.

Chapter Six

Volume, Velocity, and Complexity

"The theory of evolution by cumulative natural selection is the only theory we know of that is in principle capable of explaining the existence of organized complexity."
Richard Dawkins

Humans, like all living beings, are social by nature. They tend to congregate, communicate, argue, laugh, fight, and hug, all just to get a point across or feel as if they belong. The process of entering military service, selection and training, relies on these aspects of human nature. Military leaders and instructors leverage people's natural desire and drive to be a part of something greater, something special, a need to belong.

I was never a United States Marine, but I've led former Marines who transferred to the Navy and became SEALs. The debate over which crucible was toughest, Marine training or SEAL basic training, probably continues to rage on to this day. However, one thing I heard over and over again from these former Marines and many long serving Marine veterans over time, was that the Corps will take a young person, break down their thin veneer of feelings, thoughts, wants, needs, attitudes, and build them back up again. Adding the Marine Corp value system, pride of history, and confidence in themselves and those around them.

If this is true it sure explains a lot. The Marines are a great example of a culture defined and sustained for over two centuries without much deviation, regardless of politics, wars, religion, or advancements in war fighting technology, and they have been successful as a result of this embedded commitment to culture.

SEALs on the other hand, go through a different process. I've described it as chipping away at a lump of marble. Allowing a well-designed and sequenced series of severe physical and mental attacks, to chip away at that piece of marble until the true nature of the person within is revealed.

Sculptors seek the lines within the marble and discard the work if the marble does not expose opportunities for expression. Great art comes from the combination of the marble's interior dynamics and the skill of the sculptor's chisel. SEALs are discovered by whittling and chipping away at their surface personality to expose the confident, steady, and internally motivated man within. Course attrition due to medical issues aside, the result is a group of men, like minded and focused, who are ready to be trained and ready to win.

So, what does a discussion about the United States Marines and the SEALs have to do with this chapter? Absolutely nothing, and here's the rub. My experience in the military as a young follower, low level supervisor, mid-level manager, and combat leader was one of ease compared to what I've experienced since leaving the service. I had no idea how hard it was to find good people, train and motivate them, and lead them together to grow a successful business.

This chapter is about how to handle human nature as you find it and to do so without the benefit of tax payers handing you courageous, confident, and highly motivated people as a starting lineup. Leading change is difficult, but it is more difficult if your people can't or won't pull their weight or pull in the same direction. Over the last twenty years I've developed a personal method to evaluate my team members, leaders and supporting cast alike. I break the work into three driving forces; the volume of work stacked on a person, the velocity at which that work comes at a person, and the complexity of assigned work a person must perform.

The Peter Principle

Before I get into my three drivers of workload and the associated stress, I want to take a moment to discuss a concept conceived by Laurence J. Peter in his 1969 book, *The Peter Principle*. The key concept that made this book's main theme and its title an element in future business school curriculum was his observation of human nature and employee ability in the workplace. In short, the theory is that people tend to rise to the level of their own incompetence.

My workload, stress drivers; volume, velocity, and complexity, adhere to Lawrence Peter's principle, I've only added dimensions to his classic observation. As you read through the rest of this chapter take time to reflect on the Peter Principle and how you've seen it in action or perhaps felt its affect yourself. By adding my two cents I'm only categorizing the stress drivers so you can evaluate what is happening to your leaders, employees, or yourself.

Evaluating Work Volume

If you ask people what the number one driver of worker stress is, you'll get a variety of answers. Change, as we discussed in earlier chapters, is always near the top of the list. The other answer found near the top of the list is volume of work. People cite being "overloaded" or not compensated for the work they are required to do. Work volume can be explained in many ways, but it's usually defined by the industry and the function of the position being evaluated within an industry. Stacks of paper, widgets stamped, boxes packed, fish cleaned, complaints handled, sales made, units shipped, you get the picture.

As you think about volume as a stress driver use your own experience, past or present, to dial in your definitions. For me as a CEO it is how many strategic threats or opportunities I deal with successfully. My workflow is based on the volume of direct inputs I receive from my two operating presidents. These two channels deliver my daily demand signal.

From my perspective volume is the easiest stress or work driver to define, observe, and qualify. For example, add a two-pound plate to either side of a bar bell and eventually the number of two pound plates will add up resulting in failure for the weightlifter. Loading up an employee follows similar dynamics.

With experience a leader doesn't have to visually observe the work being done to evaluate sane workloads. They can evaluate the measured outcomes remotely, through reports, statistics, dashboards, and detect what level of effort looks reasonable, achievable, and sustainable and what level of effort does not.

Once identified, the potential for overload can be assessed by a leader using policies, written expectations, and common sense. Often the bar is set too low or too high by a leader based on faulty assumptions. A heroic employee may do the required work with less stress and perform or deliver more volume but represent only half of one percent of the company population. Set the performance bar based on this stellar worker and all others will pale in comparison.

The opposite can be true. Dumbing down the volume for a person who needs significant training or reassignment results in too low a standard. With volumes surging high and low, a moderate or adequate performance should be appropriate. Someone who can handle the ebbs and flows but steadily performs the required daily, weekly, and monthly volume. I have a high tolerance for volume and will work as long and as hard as it takes to stay ahead, catch up, or finish the to-do list in front of me. Volume is not my problem but by the end of this chapter I'll share with you what does challenge me.

Evaluating Work Velocity

How quickly a person must execute a task, or how frequently tasks hit a person, define velocity of work in the context of my experience. There is a famous episode from the old *I Love Lucy* show called *Lucy and the Chocolate Factory* (available on YouTube), where Lucy and her friend Ethel decide to take jobs wrapping small chocolate candies. In the famous skit, the two women handle things well until the conveyor belt accelerates. The velocity eventually spells disaster for the two candy workers and provides a good laugh.

As with volume, tasks can be characterized as simple or difficult. Good organizational and position design should logically take both volume and velocity of work into account. Regrettably, this is not normally the case. Planners start with good intentions, studying the workflow steps between tasks and between people or workstations. They identify the elements and subelements of each separate critical, and not so critical task, and then they assign time expectations to perform the work to their performance standard. This should be sufficient to guarantee success, but often is a shallow understanding of what is going to happen.

Once the job or task is designed job postings are created, new employees are matched to these design elements and hired, or existing employees are rotated and placed in the new positions, all based on this design approach. So why have I seen this approach not succeed in practice? There are a few reasons. One reason is evolution. Eventually, the meticulous, one time, position design effort grows stale or even obsolete. It fails to cope with an evolving new normal.

Picture in your mind a dam built to withhold a set amount of river water. Everything is fine until a subtle multi-year climate shift occurs. The spring melt always delivered a predictable amount of water to the place where the dam stands tall, protecting the valley further down. Then, one spring, a rapid torrent of water slams into the face of the dam in a short amount of time. The dam's original systems design may or may not have anticipated this climate change years in the future and it will remain to be seen if the structure can successfully bleed off the intense, non-standard flow using its control gates.

Lucy and Ethel experienced an increase in the pace of simple tasks, the challenge was speed and quality execution. The engineers who built the dam were challenged by an unexpected increase in water velocity that happens in the spring. In either example, velocity of work can destroy employee and leader morale and effectiveness as they struggle to keep up or deal with one rapidly occurring event. Some people are wired to do this well, think of air traffic controllers.

As mentioned previously, I graduated from the Navy's RADAR operator and air traffic control school before going on to SEAL training. Our starting class in RADAR school was preselected through intense aptitude and IQ testing. My classmates and I were all capable, on paper, of succeeding. At the end of course only fourteen of the original thirty students graduated. The key discriminator? You guessed it, the ability to cope with rapidly changing information, observed and graded in real time, to a strict standard, at an ever-increasing velocity of target data delivery.

Unlike work volume, challenges associated with velocity are easier to detect. In the Lucy example, velocity issues become comical and then dramatic. Velocity failure is dramatic and very public. People are seen by their coworkers failing in critical ways and the company suffers. Many times, the failure (unlike volume failure which often elicits sympathy) to handle the velocity of work makes the leader or employee appear incompetent resulting in replacement, termination, or resignation by the affected person.

The first two drivers of work stress and task management failure have each been difficult in their own way. Next, we'll tackle the subject of work complexity. By now, you've probably figured out velocity of work isn't my personal Achilles heel either.

Evaluating Work Complexity

Velocity implies a sense of acceleration, exhilaration, and trepidation. The feeling in our gut from the time we leave the plane to when the parachute finally opens above our head. Fear, excitement, and dread. Complexity of work conjures up visons of struggle, puzzle solving, and feelings of ineptitude, followed by failure. We've all succumbed to intellectual demands that are on the edge, or beyond, our capacity and competency to handle. This category of stress might be sufficient all by itself to derail your well-designed business plans.

As a CEO, many of my tasks fall into this category. Setting the volume or velocity of my complex tasks aside, just facing complex issues and doing the right thing can be exhausting. I mean, what is the right thing? A business question may sound simple and straightforward at first hearing. Then you begin to weigh the primary, secondary, and tertiary effects of one decision path against all the others.

Unintended consequences, collateral damage, relationship impact, financial impact, legal and ethical elements. Then you can add in timing. Start now, soon, later, or far in the future. Execute on your own, find a partner, or buy a company as a solution? This is my day, week, month in a nutshell.

Don't get me wrong, I'm not complaining, decision making goes with the title, so does winning and losing, except winning never seems as big a deal as losing. What is winning for me these days? As I said before, doing the right thing. Taking all the various aspects into account that make big issues challenging and complex and balancing, evaluating, and scoring them until I come to a way forward. It's scary and exhilarating at the same time. Of the three drivers, complexity is my personal leadership challenge.

Complexity can be obvious to all concerned but more often it isn't easy to see in practice. As a student learning to direct Navy aircraft my instructor couldn't see what was swirling around in my head as I juggled a dozen questions, inputs, and approved procedures, striving to arrive at a good call in sixty seconds or less. As a SEAL officer, leading men in combat my guys couldn't see my mind working the tactical problem either.

Mastering complexity is part technical training, part experience over time, and part art form. When I was younger and considered a technical expert, I had the first two of these components well in hand. The art form piece was hit and miss but I tended to make good choices, so it worked out. The older I became the more responsibility and positional authority I attained. The further up in the leadership structure I went the less my technical expertise and experience mattered. I eventually made all my complex decisions by relying on other people's knowledge and trusting in their technical acumen and judgement.

Complex work can be static and unchanging, or it can subtly evolve over time into a ball of yarn, unobserved from high above. Given enough time, most competent leaders and employees can solve complex challenges as long as the volume and velocity of their work is reasonable.

What if that isn't the case? What if in addition to a task being complex it also has a tight deadline? What if a person has five complex tasks stacked up waiting for action? Like a ticking bomb, the trusted employee steadily completes one complex task after another until suddenly they begin to fail. Are they sick? Tired? Unmotivated? Incompetent? It may be that you are the architect of their stress escalating, the quality and quantity of their work declining, and ultimately, their failure to perform.

Two or More Work Stress Drivers

Moderate work volume plus moderate work velocity and a low level of task complexity is probably the middle of the road performance benchmark we would all use to assess leaders and employees given no other information. For the sake of argument, let's say a supervisor, Tammy, has performed to standard for two years given this middle of the road benchmark regarding workload, work velocity, and task complexity. Tammy's performance is slipping and her manager notices. They discuss this change in performance and Tammy pledges to do better, to work *harder*. But things do not get better, instead they get much worse over the next six months. Tammy has had three formal counseling sessions, yet nothing has improved. What is her manager to do?

You should have an idea of where I'm going with this example. By now you are evaluating the three work stress drivers and have instinctively realized one, two, or all of them might have escalated. Since Tammy doesn't have the authority to change these factors who's to blame for her inability to handle the change? You nailed it, her manager. He or she is the person who added to Tammy's workload, added complexity, increased the demand speed in general, or decreased the amount of time Tammy had to execute her tasks.

Tammy knows these things have changed but she sees herself as responsible for performing despite the fundamental changes in her workflow. If her manager initiated the changes, he or she should be aware they did, but still refuse to rethink the job position description. If the changes came were initiated from further up the leadership ladder, the manager may sympathize with Tammy but not enough to petition her boss for a formal position evaluation and redesign, or another Tammy.

As noted earlier in this chapter, my observation is consistent as it is disturbing. Original efforts to design organizations, sub-units of organizations, and job positions, are usually sound and well-meaning. However, time works to erode this fresh design, rendering it stale and eventually obsolete.

As a leader you may find yourself at the front end of design or inserted when design logic begins to fade, and execution is declining. By thinking about the three work stress drivers in this chapter you can do your own assessment, position by position, in any type of human work structure. The receptionist is just as likely as the Vice President of Sales to suffer from workflow stress and become overwhelmed, all due to a failure of design.

I tend to walk the floor, observe reports and statistics, and ask specific questions of my leaders and employees as a regular practice, checking the pulse of the company, regularly seeing what tasks or functions are being accomplished efficiently, and which ones are not. My instincts have been honed to sharp insight over the years by doing this. A simple comment here, a subtle complaint there, a sharp joke at the expense of a coworker, they are observations that provide me with insight. When there's trouble I refer to the signs and signals as an indication the "wheels are starting to wobble".

Mentor, Intervene, Reassign, or Remove?

Depending on where you sit on the organizational chart you may or may not have authority to act on your instincts. I suggest you act anyway. In my opinion, constructive observations professionally delivered, are an obligation of every leader and employee. Think of the company as a ship at sea (I know it's a Navy thing but bear with me). Everyone relies on the ship for food, shelter, and perhaps even a source of income. Success or failure in a company affects everybody, just like on a ship. For a crewmember, no matter how junior in rank, to walk past a problem that might jeopardize the safety of the ship and crew is unheard of and is a punishable offense in the Navy.

Study the issues, dissect the workflow, and separate the employee or leader from the tasks. Determine what if anything has changed and when it changed. Like a murder mystery, the first person accused often isn't the killer. Intervene to redesign the position, the work, or both and then train the leader or employee to the new normal. Sometimes being nimble is simply being honest and open minded. Act on your instincts!

Chapter Seven

The 85% Rule

"85% ready is good enough, if you're 85% of the way there, then make the decision to go for it. Hesitation doesn't do anybody any good."
Charles Schwab

The pursuit of perfection has killed a million ideas, hopes, and dreams. Most of us believe attaining perfection in school, sports, a hobby, marriage, parenthood, and professionally is the goal of the game. I'm here to tell you that it is not. The pursuit of perfection begins at a fast pace, everything is a go, and the end feels achievable, inevitable. Then reality pushes back. Momentum slows, traction wanes, and friction increases. The timeline for completion, perfection, invariably gets pushed further into the future.

Don't get me wrong, there are a few things we'd all like to see performed to perfection, brain surgery for one, piloting a commercial airliner is another. However, most of human activity and goal-based effort is not associated with such dire life and death possibilities. As a rule, we try, but fall short of perfection. This chapter contains insights that will provide you with a free pass to fall short of perfect and feel good about doing so. In business and in life, getting most of the way there is sufficient. Understanding that is a key to being and staying nimble, I'll explain.

You are Burning Daylight

SEAL senior enlisted leaders barked out quite a few sayings, mottos, and sage words to live by as they motivated their men to complete a task. One of my favorites was related to wasting time. "Strong! You're burning daylight!" I would stop thinking about the chore and start performing the chore when I heard this loud admonishment. Time is always critical, thinking deep thoughts requires time, planning great projects takes time, and execution takes time. If you learn to master time you will be successful. Yes, wasting time can increase performance stress and begin to pile up overdue tasks. In this reality, rest, fun, and personal learning get squeezed out of the schedule.

Time can be important in other ways, too. Seizing a window of opportunity is a matter of judgement combined with speed of action. This should be a rule of business physics taught in every business school. A line from a 1712 play, *Cato*, by John Addison, sums it up well, *he who hesitates is lost*.

An example of this principle can be found by looking at the plight of U.S. aircrews and pilots shot down during the Vietnam War. The failure to rescue most of the pilots shot down over Vietnam wasn't due to a lack of trying, a lack of material resources, or the lack of men courageous enough to make the attempt.

The failure was due to over-analysis. Too much time spent focused on perfect risk mitigation. Fear of failure led to the creation of multiple layers of rescue mission approvals (this was determined in studies conducted long after that war ended). Time and time again a pilot would eject, float to earth, signal his readiness to be picked up, and then wait until captured. These poor souls waited in vain, first on the ground standing next to their parachute and then, later, in prisoner of war camps.

Rescuing pilots and air crews was recognized by everybody as a high priority in Vietnam, from the commanding general all the way down the chain of command. The sad result of systemic handwringing over perfection was a low number of successful rescues from 1962 to 1975. There is another well-worn term that fits this example, *paralysis by analysis*. The desire, the drive, or the mandate that every element involved in a decision must be accounted for, scrutinized, and weighed, before making a commitment to action. No doubt you've observed this behavior in your own business.

The reality is windows of opportunity open and close without warning and the length of time they will stay open is unknown. Being a nimble leader is being a courageous leader. Have faith in your judgement. Walk away on purpose, not because there isn't enough time to study the opportunity, or act on purpose. Seize the moment. It's discouraging to know that many leaders will not jump through that window due to an overabundance of caution, multi-layered authority matrixes, decision methodology driven first and foremost by risk avoidance. In my experience there are a variety of opportunities in life and in business. I'll focus on three that appear in business, tactical, operational and strategic opportunity.

A Tactical Window of Opportunity

Tactical decisions are important. They are near if not actually real time calls, and they add up, the good ones and the bad. Tactical opportunities are defined by short duration windows when going left instead of right is the difference between success and failure, albeit with lower consequences for failure than operational and strategic missteps. As a SEAL I lived in a high- stakes, high speed, high consequence tactical world. Going left or right might mean the difference between life and death.

As a leader, directing a SEAL to go right or left meant you might have to live with the negative consequences of your decisions. In business leadership, you might have an opportunity to create a teaching moment, a mentoring exercise, or an opportunity to hit the pause button and conduct some desperately needed training. Those tactical windows open and close daily.

The key to seizing this important window of opportunity

is awareness. Start each morning looking through your task list and when you're finished, mentally walk through the day you have planned. See yourself interacting with your leaders, technical experts, and support personnel. Picture these people in your mind's eye and then add a few new items to your task list. Prioritize the fleeting tactical opportunities provided to you every day to influence the small behaviors, to motivate, to observe. Pursue these tactical objectives with the same dedication you devote to the other daily tasks. This process works, try it, you'll see!

If you understand this concept let's take it a step further. Train your subordinate leadership to practice proactive tactical decision making. Guide them to become better, smarter, and more impactful. Don't neglect the needs of your boss either. He or she may not be enlightened to the powerful idea of seizing these small, daily windows of opportunity. Tactfully guide them and you'll be pleasantly surprised as they become more attuned to reality.

An Operational Window of Opportunity

Formal planning activity conducted by most leaders lives at the operational level of engagement. In fact, most leaders devote all their planning efforts to that intermediate time frame, beyond day to day effort but short of addressing strategic horizons. Windows of opportunity at this level of leadership are calculated and often a series of choices between competing imperatives. Should I execute project A or Project B? Now? Later? In parallel?

I've found that many leaders are capable of planning at the operational level even though these same diligent leaders miss tactical opportunities and more often, ignore the strategic ones. Leadership training programs do a decent job of preparing leaders at all levels how to plan, prepare, and execute operational activities. This skill set is valuable in a slow to moderately paced environment but in a fast-moving industry the plodding, hyper detailed operational planning mindset is often overwhelmed by reality, a reality shaped by the economy, the market or industry, or the competition.

If you find this happening to you it might be time to shorten the operational planning process to accommodate the speed of your business and the changing landscape affecting that same business. It may be time to put together a good plan you can execute instead of a perfect plan that is moot before it's even fully implemented.

Here's something to consider. Weigh your operational opportunities, execute what you can when you can and spend at least four hours a week developing an appreciation for the world, your market, the state of competition, beyond those operational plans. Learn to think strategically and then plan operations further and further out toward the far horizon. In your industry that may be a six month horizon or much longer. One thing to consider, when you reach the point where you can no longer fill your operational planning template with quality data, stop. You've likely arrived at the threshold of strategic planning.

A Strategic Window of Opportunity

In 2015, I was a newly minted CEO responsible for creating a way forward, a strategic vision that took into account our corporate strengths and weaknesses, contemplated potential opportunities over the next few years, and set a course through that unknown future to a successful outcome. Strategic thinking can be stimulating, intellectually satisfying, even fun. In fact, my most enthusiastic executives enjoy spending time discussing what the future holds.

I learned how to think strategically when assigned to a small strategy group created in late 1989 to figure out the role of Navy special warfare in support of the U.S. Special Operations Command. What missions would SEALs do and where would the line be drawn between our responsibilities and those of the Army and Air Force special operations commands? How should our Navy's special capabilities evolve? Would we be technology driven? Would the SEAL teams shift emphasis to nation building like their Army Green Beret brethren or would we reduce the scope of our capabilities to focus solely on the beach and harbor environments and leave the fight ashore to the Marines?

There were no clear answers, but I sensed a vacuum that presented us with an opportunity. The consolidated special operations command was formed in the mid-1980's but they didn't flex their muscles until 1990. The opportunity to put our vision on paper quickly and beat a higher echelon entity (the Pentagon, the new Special Operations Command, or the Department of the Navy) from deciding for us, was closing so we got to work.

I devoted half my day to this effort for a year and generated a considerable number of white papers, thought pieces outlining how SEALs could and should shape our future. This was an audacious point of view for a junior naval officer. My win rate was low, but I did help to influence the future, but as time passed many of my rejected insights turned out to be correct.

I guess I've always had a knack for the vision thing, the strategy group in the Navy was just the beginning. But learned that planning and thinking about the future is much easier than being personally or professionally responsible for the plan's execution and outcome. I found this out years later when I began to build business strategies at the division level inside companies.

What success I've had developing strategy isn't due to an ability to craft lofty, inspirational narratives. It is due instead to my ability to see the strategic opportunity and my willingness to take the leap. I've often wondered why others don't perform well when divining the future of a business, a market, or an industry. Fear of failure is one limiting factor. Who wants to be the blowhard that predicts wild success thirty-six months out and then fails to achieve the vision? Strategy is high stakes risk taking, especially when you must commit limited resources to the long term plan. Being wrong is more than failing to succeed, it may also mean you've allowed your competitors to leapfrog you in the marketplace or render your company obsolete. You must have the fortitude to risk potential failure on a grand scale.

Great battles, the ones that determine the outcome of a war, the fate of a nation, are rare these days. They are, however, a study in human decision making on a scale that rises above mere life and death to the destruction or preservation of a way of life. My study of historic strategic battles reveals that being willing to act within the limited period a strategic window of opportunity stays open and it is a key element of strategic leadership and victory. The length of time the opportunity to act exists defines the "window." Hesitate too long and the window closes.

Battles evolve months, weeks, days, and hours before armies engage in combat. Often the strategic decision making is simply a victim of fate once battle commences. In modern companies coherent and opportunistic businesses strategy is no less critical to success. Business leaders are no less susceptible than heads of state and generals to hesitation and fear of failure. Think about this. Every day in America and around the world, windows of strategic business opportunity open and close without notice, or if noticed, without decisive action by business leaders. In my opinion, the eighty-five percent rule is at play here.

Strategic risk mitigation taken to the extreme, demands zero exposure to risk. Zero tolerance for failure. Many leaders know viscerally what risk represents. It represents pain, potential demotion, or even termination. For that reason, leaders often, decline opportunities that do not present a slam dunk proposition for easy, risk-free success.

No strategic opportunity is without downside and a reluctance to leap through the window of opportunity is directly related to the point of this chapter. The drive to have perfect knowledge, to plan perfectly, to mitigate risk perfectly, is the drive that ignores possibilities and seeks to clear away all doubt, not maximize opportunity. See the window, take the leap, apply logic and insight until you are eighty-five percent sure and then, as the company Nike says, just do it!

Time Travel

The eighty-five percent rule is easier to write about than to adopt as a leadership style. Time is the issue. We live in the past, trending past behaviors and activities forward. We average the past and make assumptions about our future. We live in the moment and project that moment into the future. The eighty-five percent rule requires a bit of time travel to be useful. It also requires a dose of confidence and a little faith.

At the tactical level you should see be able to spot the opening, to see it unfold in the moment. Should you seize the initiative or ignore the opening? Should you note the observed tactical issue but develop a larger operational approach to address shortcomings or opportunities? Is the observed behavior a precursor of larger, long term problems in your organization? Does it rise to the level of strategic value or criticality?

I refer to time travel because that's what a bias for action feels like when I perform this leadership exercise. I see in my mind's eye a projection of the past, a line of familiar information extending into the near term (operational landscape) and farther out into the future, my leadership horizon (strategic landscape).

As a strategic exercise, I test a line of business logic by playing with it, manipulating the possibilities and probabilities. Does the assumptive logic of the past make sense? Has the past truly been prologue to the present? Then I run trial lines of future outcomes, categorizing them into three buckets. Things get worse, things stay the same, and things get better. I envision what might happen to our business, our market, even our industry, for each future track.

This time travel method allows you to virtually experience the effects of several futures, both positive and negative. I tend to ignore the static outcome track and focus on designing strategic plans that deal with the better, and worse than expected paths. As you plan you should identify challenges; challenges to changing group think, impact on existing plans, and availability of resources.

This works at the tactical and operational level of thought and action as well. I often perform the time travel exercise real time, to determine if a tactical opportunity exists. I see the window, project back then forward, contemplating history, the present circumstances, and what could be, then I act and deliver the appropriate guidance, on the spot. If immediate action isn't reasonable, I complete the initial time travel experience and as soon as possible afterward, try to write down the probable, possible, and the impossible futures I've conjured up.

Time travel allows you to draft the future and load the draft with insights and questions to be answered. Opportunities come in two flavors: threat identification and protective action and growth identification and accretive action. Dodging a threat is just as important as creating a new product or service that makes your company an industry leader.

Load your draft up with resource costs required to either avoid or to seize what you perceive might be coming your way. Calculate the timeline and the speed or pace of change. Factor in what steps are necessary to prepare and when they need to happen. Finally, bounce your perceptions against your existing formal plans and assumptions about the future. How do they stand up? Are they all positively oriented without considering threats to success? Do they address opportunities to win thoroughly, comprehensively, or are they lacking? Do your plans lean forward, grounded in reality, or do they reflect a mirror image of the past carried forward?

I've explained this exercise hundreds of times and the same questions always comes up. When do you schedule time to perform the time travel exercise? What format do you use to collect your thoughts? How do you chunk the future into blocks of time to conduct your analysis? The questions themselves reveal a desire to lock down the variables, to format, organize, and lock down the unknown the future represents. I suggest a creative and nimble journey first. Once you see the path toss the mechanics to a project manager or a finance officer. Your job is to lead, and vision is a key character trait in successful leaders.

My answers to these questions never satisfy. I perform the exercise every day, often near continuously during the day. I takes notes, draw dry erase board diagrams, sketch out ideas, but I never use a fixed, defined format. The very practice of using templates and formats restricts and channels creative impulses and insights converting revelation into inputs. Free thought and daydreaming can be enlightening. Capture the gist and come back to the notes to evaluate the need for action later. Think, create, and then build.

The Speed of Business

The speed of business, any business, has accelerated to a point most leaders live in a reactionary world. Overloaded with analysis, confronted with piles of work waiting to be completed, many leaders can't spare the time to look up from the to-do list to dream, explore, and wonder. In the world of business, reality flies by like a stealth fighter. Swift, vague, and threatening. Here one second and gone the next. How do you catch lightning in a bottle?

In the end, perfection is both a curse and an illusion. You need to step back and take stock. Are you struggling to attain false and unattainable goals? Are your projects evolving continuously in response to a rapidly changing business environment? If so, understand that this is the symptom of static thought and unimaginative leadership. I can't slow it down for you, you will have to change your paradigm and adapt.

All plans are rapid prototyping structures. They must be agile and malleable. In addition to this new planning mindset you will need to match your personal learning curve to the change profile. Become the leader you will have to be in the future, but do it now, don't wait. Seize the day, do not seek perfection, and do not adopt risk mitigation as your mantra. Be bold, be quick, and be humble. It's time to start sprinting! Forget pursuit of perfection. Your forward leaning bias for action, risk tolerance, and visionary journey begins now!

Chapter Eight

Wisdom Through Experimentation

> *"Whether you're shuffling a deck of cards or holding your breath, magic is pretty simple: It comes down to training, practice, and experimentation, followed up by ridiculous pursuit and relentless perseverance."*
> **David Blaine**

Constructive creativity differs from brainstorming or random acts of artistic fancy by a focus on useful outcomes. The goal isn't beauty for beauty's sake, or poetic bliss. Constructive creativity aims to achieve tangible results through tangential or asymmetrical thinking.

A study of great innovators in industry, regardless of the type of industry, reveals that innovation, and that rarer cousin, invention, are often the positive outcome of experimentation. Trial and error, repeated attempts to arrive at the functional threshold of effective application, and failure, is a natural part of creative experimentation.

From my personal experience, this process of failing repeatedly is emotional. Not in the sobbing I lost my girlfriend or boyfriend way, but in a way that chips away at your passion and positive outlook. To be a nimble leader is to be a creative leader and if you are to be truly creative, you must live through the crucible of failure to win. Whatever winning is for you or your company.

Experimentation is formal, the process of working through a challenge through insight and observation to achieve a result. Experimentation also provides us with the opportunity to fail and failing imparts more wisdom than success. Baseball Hall of Fame slugger Babe Ruth is a classic example of this reality.

In his career he established amazing statistics for runs batted in and home runs, the gold standard of hitting performance. Babe Ruth also held the league's strike out record. He knew that with every missed ball he was becoming smarter, *wiser*. The rest is baseball history.

The Case for Risk Taking

Here we are again, discussing the single greatest impediment to nimble leadership and creative thinking in general; risk taking. It's a cliché but the fear of failure paradigm is real. Countless studies suggest this fear is much stronger than our desire to win or gain something of value. Humans in general are more likely to choose safety over personal gain if that choice involves any risk to themselves physically, or risk to their status. Leaders are no exception to this paradigm.

Look at the greatest leaders of history, in art, war, business, and science. Alexander the Great, Leonardo Di Vinci, Michelangelo, Napoleon, Albert Einstein, Steve Jobs, and others were all young when they created their breakthroughs. Much of the rest of their lives were spent living up to their early creative successes. Why do you think this happens? I believe it was their naive, youthfully optimistic, and openminded attitude toward risk taking.

Young people have less to lose materially, less personal status at risk, and they do not have a long list of failures to dissuade them from challenging the world. This isn't biological as much as it is psychological. An older person is also capable of thinking wild thoughts and taking great risks, however most don't. So, it appears to be more a mindset thing. That's the good news if you are older than thirty years old. There are examples of this elder energy; Elon Musk and Sir Richard Branson, to name two. If your risk tolerance is tied to retaining your title, your material wealth, or your job, you will be reluctant to experiment because to experiment you must fail to win.

Leaders Lead – Managers Manage

Today's professional manager evolved from an ancient caste system of opportunistic merchants and government bureaucrats uniquely positioned to administer to the affairs of the wealthy or ruling class. This is still the case in many underdeveloped countries but in more sophisticated capitalist nations learning to become a manager is a vocation.

Now, professional managers are created. They are educated and groomed through an assembly line of colleges and universities dedicated to imparting standardized terms, appropriate historical references, selected case studies, and approved role definitions. Professional management training is directed at producing scores of newly minted junior managers, ready to be plugged into a modern company.

There are still examples of managers working their way up the ladder, doing it all through on the job training, but they too are being held to the standards and traditions dictated by the norms of professional management. One of the things formally trained and on the job managers have in common is that neither were taught that taking risks is a good thing. So, what is the point in calling this truth out? Simple, you need to know the difference between being a professional manager and being a leader.

When I was in Baghdad, Iraq in 2004 supporting the U.S. State Department, I was responsible for hundreds of highly trained professionals tasked with protecting the U.S. Ambassador and several high-ranking U.S. officials. We had many pithy and insightful slogans and common sense operating procedures. These were the simple truths, developed by men who placed themselves between a VIP and an assassin's bullet or bomb, every day. One of these maxims was d*rivers drive, shooters shoot, and leaders lead.*

When I first heard this phrase, I didn't get it. I appeared to be so simple and obvious a directive that it didn't have value. Then someone explained it to me, and I saw the light. When normal people, in normal jobs, become stressed self-preservation drives odd behavior aimed at self-preservation.

When former elite special operations operators, Marines, and Rangers come under stress in battle they all want to act, to save the day. The simple maxim was repeated in the morning briefings in Baghdad, and again inside each armored sedan over the radio as the protective teams left the safety of the American Green Zone. The message was focus on *your* assigned task. If each of the team members do this, everything will run smoothly, and we will get ourselves, and the VIP back safely. The alternative is heroic chaos and worse. This principal worked in conditions of incredible stress. How can you apply it to business leadership?

In my opinion and based on my years of experience as both a manager and a leader the distinction is clear. I've performed in both roles, alternating back and forth as I changed jobs or as I was elevated within large corporations. I know intuitively they are two different positions with different duties and responsibilities. Why then has this distinction become blurred to the point the job of manager and leader are nearly synonymous?

Managers manage. My definition of management is straightforward; managers manage systems and processes and the human resources associated with those systems and processes. The performance metrics and the performance path are clearly delineated. Managers must follow policies and procedures. Protocols, rules, and regulations are put in place to maintain (and here's the punchline) order. We need great managers but being a manager doesn't qualify you to be a leader.

Breaking Glass

When I was a young SEAL there was a cartoon depicting a SEAL combat doll, fully covered in weapons and bullets, camouflaged from head to toe, wearing a stern look. This doll stood on a pedestal, covered in a clear glass shell. The caption of the cartoon read; *U.S. Navy SEAL – break glass in case of war*. This was only a few years after the end of the Vietnam War, but the cartoon was already sending the wrong message. The Navy was cleaning up its act. Clean uniforms and clean-shaven warriors were the standard again, gone were the loose, cowboy antics of the wartime SEALs.

I confess, I enjoyed those early years, but I wasn't consciously aware of why the combat veterans scorned many of the rules and restrictions, both during, and immediately after the war. In the early 1980s everything changed. We entered a new phase, a managed phase of evolution.

Following the rules didn't make us better, it just made the senior brass happy. By 1982 we were no longer a risk factor to be monitored. Businesses and even non-profit organizations go through this cycle of loose, tight, loose, and tight cultural change. I began to wonder why one or the other condition wasn't adhered to all the time. Why did organizations swing from one extreme to the other, culturally?

I've come to the conclusion that challenges, true challenges, are defined by their power to disrupt or defeat the status quo posture. Standards, rules, procedures, these are useful concepts, but they are historical footnotes of the way the last set of challenges were handled. They are rarely flexible or forward looking and that's how businesses get tripped up. In this situation what can a manager to do?

The existing systems and processes, maybe even the people are failing to cope. This is when leadership, not management, is needed. This is the moment when you can define leadership by your actions to build. It's time to break glass and let loose the warrior!

Do we still require managers? The answer is yes. We need managers even in crisis. You will need good managers to maintain the status quo while you focus on solving the challenge and build the solution. You'll require managers to implement your solution and then, that's right, manage the new status quo.

Leaders step up to face chaos and crisis brought about by a failure of existing capabilities and capacity to handle the issue at hand. Leaders are going to assess the challenges objectively and analyze possible solutions before breaking conventions by applying those solutions, regardless of their misalignment with existing norms. A manager who is comfortable with this is a manager with true leadership potential. A manager who is willing to step away from the rules and create a new path to success is in fact, a leader.

When they are needed, we are all wise to let leaders lead and managers manage. Task focus, task resource, solve the crisis, survive the chaos, and then let the managers clean up the mess and document the new way of doing things. Sounds easy, right? It doesn't actually happen this way very often. The reason is simple, there are very few true leaders among us.

I have watched this play out in the military, the investment world, politics, and in business. I've pinpointed the reason why leaders are rare, and it might surprise you. I contend that there are many potential leaders all around us, every day. People who, for whatever reason, can step up and make the right things happen when others are in a state of shock. The sticking point is risk, personal risk.

Most companies are "led" by managers happy to wait "while Rome burns," assured by their faith in systems and processes that their management team will prevail. These senior "leaders" will not tolerate, support, or endorse true leadership. It feels too much like vandalism. True leadership requires courage, creativity, poise, and a willingness to take risks. Sadly, taking risks isn't how most senior managers ascend to the top of their companies. They ascend by not rocking the boat.

Avoiding or eliminating risk was the way senior management made their way to the top. To these folks, true leaders are a virus whose open mindedness, creativity, and wanton disregard for the rules and traditions, mark them as a threat. True leaders are treated as a violation of collective wisdom. Heretics unwilling to shut up and sit down. In most cases they are certainly not encouraged. Management is responsible for, to steal a military phase, good order and discipline. They will not let a leader's personality disrupt that good order. This is especially prevalent in large companies and corporations.

This is a book about nimble leadership, creative leadership, bold leadership. Understanding management science is important but good leaders pay for their keep by staying on their toes not sitting in their cubicles. Good leaders are willing to trend forward, to investigate flaws in their systems, processes, and overall business methodology.

Good leaders are routinely good managers. They surveil their daily activity, as required, to standard, while from time to time staring out of the window toward a far off horizon, wondering "what if?" They carve out a piece of their day to look for potential threats and opportunities and they continuously test their existing structure to confirm alignment with reality and crisis survivability. If they find fault, they fix, repair, upgrade, or overhaul *in advance of the challenge*. If you already doing these things, congratulations! You are thinking like a leader. I suggest you use the tools and concepts in this book to further your development and understanding. If you are not thinking like a leader, what's stopping you? This book can show you the way to grow beyond management. If you embrace leadership, you will find yourself better prepared and positioned for the day you need to step up and lead. Trust me, that day is coming.

Experimentation and Creative Leadership

In 1993, the Navy decided to shut down its mini-submarine program for lack of use. The program included not only the highly technical minisubs but also shelters, hangar like structures mounted on U.S. submarine decks to house, launch, and recover the small vessels. SEALs had been used in wars large and small since their inception in 1962, but the expensive mini submarines had barely seen the light of day during these conflicts. I was asked to write a position paper, explaining how the SEALs might use the vessels. If I was successful, we might receive a reprieve from the inevitable. My task put simply was to find a relevant, modern application for the minisubs. The catch was, I'd never seen a minisub let alone ridden in or driven one.

As it turned out it was my very ignorance and openminded approach to the challenge that became the key. I couldn't help but see the two-decade old program from a different perspective. I wrote the paper, and my recommendations were sufficiently helpful that the program's immediate demise was postponed.

That wasn't the end. Soon after hearing of this success I was directed to report immediately to one of the two SEAL commands that specialized in this minisub capability. I was given a one-year probationary period to prove that what I'd put down on paper was feasible. Upon arrival at the minisub team, I pulled a group of young SEALs together. They were all qualified to "fly" the minisubs but were too new to the SEAL teams to have established closed minds. They would be perfect for the task at hand and prove the Navy wrong.

I gave the men my commander's intent and told them the three things (as told to me by all the experts) preventing successful use of the minisubs. Six hours later I was summoned to a large building in the SEAL compound where these young SEALs proudly walked me through their solution to each of the three challenges.

I was stunned. They had solved issues deemed impossible by engineers and senior Navy research experts yet there it was. They had experimented in parallel all day with a competition to see who had the best answer to each of the three dilemmas.

Rapid experimentation, rapid prototyping using two by fours and PVC pipes and in six hours these young men changed naval history. Within a year the Navy was convinced and all minisub operations followed the new path. These incredible machines are still in use to this day.

In 2009, I was President and Chief Operating Officer of a rapidly growing defense company. I was faced with the choice of using conventional organizational structures and adding expensive full-time employees, using less expense independent contractors, or creating a third option, a hybrid approach. I chose to reinvent our conventional organizational structure by adopting a formation that was proven to be successful in design studios and large creative content companies. It went by many names but the name I liked was, *the cluster.*

The cluster was a jelly fish, no hard lines, no silos. Everybody was cross qualified in everything and when it was ready it provided me with a five-dimensional team. I could rotate the group to focus on business development leveraging eighty to one hundred percent of my assigned brain power. I could rotate the focus toward recruiting and onboarding new contract employees, logistics research, acquisition, and supply chain management, or I could focus them on project management.

At first this was concept confusing. Everybody wanted the safety and security of a title and a lane of responsibility, not to mention guarantees regarding where they would sit (I'm not kidding). But very shortly after implementation, morale didn't only improve, it soared.

Everybody became invested in success of every shape and size and everybody loved the new culture of multi-talented partners collaborating to beat the odds, the timetable, or just self imposed goals. By using this approach, we were able to grow rapidly without adding expensive layers of new labor. In time we became so efficient we doubled the size of the company. We didn't need to add new people, and we allowed natural employee attrition to lean out the cluster without adverse effect.

Tentanda Via Est - The Way Must be Tried

A few years ago, my grown children conspired to give me a Christmas gift, something I didn't have or even contemplated having. They bought me a DNA test so I could discover everything about my Irish heritage. The test was simple and a week or so later I received the results by email. I was surprised to say the least. My maternal grandmother was from Ireland and owned and operated the only Irish pub in Sioux City, Iowa for forty years before her passing. My dad's side was English, a little German and Irish. Simple deduction, I was Irish American. Not true according to the test.

According to the test I'm actually sixty-five percent Scandinavian and French with only a smattering of Irish and English. I was never one to research my family tree, but this outcome intrigued me. After a few months of digging I had a good picture of where the Strong's originated and why I was mostly Scandinavian and French. I discovered my name was a deviation of a Norman name, a name associated with William the Conqueror's invasion and conquest of England in the year 1066. Later, in Norman dominated England, the hated invaders dropped the French *le* in front of their names and le Strange became Stronge.

Why does this have any bearing on our discussion about leadership and creativity? Maybe it doesn't, but I found, aside from a Templar ancestor in the second Crusade, a coat of arms with the family motto; Tentanda Via Est, *the way must be tried!* Well, this suited my life experience perfectly. Without planning to, I'd lived a life of risk taking and exploration. The family motto said it all. A genetic mandate over eight hundred years old!

To be creative you must be willing to explore and learn, be humble enough to be paranoid, and be willing to peer into the future and anticipate the unknown. In practical terms you, and your team of leaders, managers, and employees, need to become comfortable with chaos, not fear it. Lean into the horizon and prepare for the fight that is surely coming. If you do this, I believe you will be surprised at how resilient and resourceful you and your business will become. You will not freeze, and you will not quit when challenged. If your instincts tell you to act, to evolve, do it! The way must be tried!

Learning from your Mistakes

Wisdom represents the sum of your personal mistakes, but you can expand on this by becoming an avid student of biographies. Gaining insights and wisdom by studying other people's mistakes and understanding how they persevered in the end is a great way to grow professionally. I still read about leaders and I don't distinguish between life or business lessons learned by a Gandhi compared to a Steve Jobs. All leadership lessons matter and impart wisdom.

If you want to be nimble you will need to embrace experimentation and the risk that comes with it. This may require you to find an environment where experimentation and creative solutions are not just tolerated but encouraged. You know my thoughts on risk taking and the role it plays psychologically when leaders face challenges. Try to convince your superiors that experimentation and risk taking are keys to excellence. If they still don't agree, move on to more fertile pastures, or start your own adventure!

Chapter Nine

Creative Planning

"We cannot solve our problems with the same thinking we used when we created them."
Albert Einstein

I could write an entire book on planning. I've spent most of my professional life learning to plan, developing plans, and executing plans. Sometimes successfully, other times not so much. In the late 1960s business schools became enamored of engineering project or process management. Linear, detailed, and easy to understand, a project timeline could be loaded with resource demands, time per activity, and collective project time requirements. Today, project management is a prerequisite for sound management. However, despite its practical allure, this chapter is not about touting the efficiency and efficacy, of project management.

Commander's Intent

The U.S. Army has a concept they teach soldiers and officers referred to as commander's intent. This concept is simple, easy to grasp, and remarkably effective. It goes like this. A team of say, ten soldiers and one officer are given the mission to patrol to a key bridge located on the edge of the battlefield and establish a defensive position there. The intent of the mission is to prevent enemy forces from using this bridge. The team is to control the bridge for forty-eight hours or until relieved by a larger friendly force.

On the way to the bridge the team is attacked by an enemy scouting party and the team's leader is severely wounded. The second in command, a senior sergeant, rallies his men and continues moving toward the bridge. When he arrives there, he discovers the enemy has placed four soldiers on the bridge to hold it open for their use. A fight ensues and the sergeant is killed taking the position from the enemy. The next in line, a corporal, takes charge and informs his headquarters that his team is in possession of the bridge. The corporal holds the bridge until relieved by a larger force ten hours later.

Commander's intent is the process of communicating the core purpose of an action, a plan, or even a strategy, to everyone carrying out those activities, and I mean everyone. Fighting enemy soldiers in general, wasn't the intent of the team's mission. Watching the bridge from a distance wasn't the team's mission either. In this example, every person on that patrol knew the point of the mission and knew it was the team's responsibility, not only the responsibility of their officer.

This may sound too simple to be valuable, but you'll find that many businesses do not communicate the driving purpose behind their daily grind. Most militaries around the world do not practice commander's intent believing their junior leaders and enlisted troops are too unsophisticated or too untrustworthy to carry on a critical mission without micromanagement and supervision by an elite, hand-picked officer.

So, what does this have to do with creative planning? Everything. Any plan, creative or not so creative, fails in execution. Commander's intent is a smart way to invigorate your leaders and your employees. A way to ensure everybody is aware of the end game, the key performance metrics, and the reasons they are spending precious time and scarce resources on the project. Be nimble is all about creativity and applying creativity to all aspects of leadership. Commander's intent is a useful way to keep everybody on their toes and leaning forward.

It Comes Back to Training

The SEALs, and all elite military organizations, train all the time. Training for these units is believed to be the differentiator on the battlefield. This holds true for professional sports. Out train an equally talented opponent and you usually beat them. The famous Rocky series of movies leverage this theme. A regular mug from the mean streets of Philadelphia has few skills but a ton of heart. How can he possibly prevail over finely tuned professional athletes? You guessed it; he trains harder. Training becomes the difference for Rocky Balboa between victory and defeat.

So, why don't businesses train as hard as Rocky? Is it arrogance? Do they feel so powerful and dominant they can do no wrong, never lose a fight? How about the leaders? How about you? When was the last time you sat down and inventoried your strengths and weaknesses?

We covered this drill in depth early in the book, but it bears repeating. Creativity in planning begins with a focus on the little things. Are your graphics state of the art? Are your financial systems generating accurate data analysis? Do you have planning software that contemplates the complexity and demands of the new plan? Or are you beginning the fight stale, underpowered, using beer math and PowerPoint shapes to create your manifesto?

In my experience, nimble leaders are creative leaders, and as creative leaders they are in a near state of continuous planning. In early 2009, I joined a small defense contracting company. The founder (we became partners later), asked me to create a strategy for his company. He wanted me to do this *before* I became too familiar with the company and its limitations. I went to work immediately.

My first task was to evaluate the market, both opportunities and competitive threats. I also studied the federal government as a customer, first in its entirety, and then focused only on the defense department. I reviewed the company's website and the marketing material to understand the brand message. Then I performed a white board exercise to plot all the business vectors and where they intersected with my new company. I produced a one-page executive summary and handed it to my new boss. He was thrilled and directed me to build an audacious business plan to get us where my strategic plan said we could be someday.

I still have that one-page strategy and occasionally, I pull it out to see how close we've come to that vision. Eleven years later I'm happy to say we've far exceeded our wildest expectations based on that one-page list of dreams. My audacious business plan was all about training, cross training, and promoting cross trained and multi-faceted performers upward to more senior, more influential, positions in the company as we grew.

Growing and scaling in this manner limited the need for expensive new hires, forged a culture of cooperation, and converted all involved into a cohesive winning machine. The goals of that early business plan would never have been met without the intense commitment to a training discipline. Are you building and honing your team's planning skills?

Baby Steps

I've observed master planners, people gifted with vision, seeing a probable future in every detail. Few if any of these architects of change were masterful at project management and the nimble leadership required to turn a plan into reality. You do not have to be a genius to create a masterful outcome. In fact, being a genius might be detrimental to seeing all the options available.

The term baby steps were used in the SEALs for advanced training in high acuity activities and tasks requiring precise physical skill. Each SEAL operator represented a list of capabilities and limitations and the sum of these attributes, comprising a two, four, eight, or twenty-man SEAL unit, was a homogenization of these individual operator traits.

The baby steps concept worked like this; first you evaluate capabilities and shortfalls, then you match the evaluation against specific standards of individual performance. Next, you create a personalized plan of corrective training to achieve as nearly as possible, similar operator profiles of superior performance. When this was complete you applied the same process to the team collectively, regardless of size. The team standards and performance requirements were complex but relied directly on the individual performance contributions of each man.

The second application of baby steps is in the detailed training process itself. Each mental and physical task is broken down, like one would do adhering to standard project management work break down schedules. No single SEAL operator would progress to the next micro step until they'd mastered the current one. This means no generic or group training sessions. Think about all the kids left behind in math when in public school they teach at a pace that must be maintained or you fall behind. Not because of aptitude, but because the material is moving at a pace set by teachers with little regard to the *learners* needs.

The baby steps approach is tedious to design and to implement execute but it produces superior results. SEALs and other special operations units swear by this process. If you are committed to being a great planner and a great plan leader you need to commit the time to prepare yourself and your planning team. All the people involved, however slightly, should be run through a baby steps training event before sitting down to create a plan or execute one. The method produces sharpness, a keen edge. It works!

When people are tightly dialed in from the start of the planning process their confidence is rock solid, they are energetic, and they are ready to explore the art of the possible. They conduct a more insightful analysis of the external environment, and produce a more honest appraisal of your organization's strengths and weaknesses. It's hard for people to be creative and open to new ideas when, like our sad sixth grader, they were left behind from the beginning.

Hive Planning

I have regular debates with my younger leaders about crowd this and crowd that. Don't get me wrong, leveraging as many brain cells as possible to solve problems or design solutions makes good business sense. Napoleon Hill, author of the greatest self-help book of all time, *Think and Grow Rich*, referred to crowdsourcing knowledge as tapping into the "master mind".

Although published in 1937, Hill was aware of the power of humility as he searched for truth and insight. He described a story of personal progressive enlightenment based on his interviews with the most successful business leaders in America at the time. Crowdsourcing ideas and using networked information channels to increase the volume of insights is a sound philosophy. Crowdsourcing decisions, in my opinion, is not a sound philosophy. This is where I break with today's misuse of the crowd sourcing concept.

I've watched a stream of young employees and leaders grab hold of networking and socialized research and use it as intended, to expand horizons, enlist experts, and improve analytic assumptions. This method is hammered into students in today's institutions of higher learning and then reinforced in corporate America. What these young, enthusiastic people are not being taught is how to decide. How to take the risk, take action, *after* the big data collection, insightful study, and final risk mitigation analysis. Instead, many apply crowdsourcing to decision making and invent a new animal, shared accountability.

Shared accountability, absent a designated and accountable leader, is an expression of professional, social, or personal risk mitigation. Any plan decided upon in this manner will be laced with compromise, not excellence. Devoid of bold risks, edgy and provocative solutions. It will be homogenized, neutered, and bland. And if it fails, who's to blame? No one.

I like the idea of creating a hive mentality. It goes with the cultural training mentioned earlier. A culture of evolving and ever improving professionals, nurtured by the company, and drilled in candid, project plan design methodology. Letting the facts speak for themselves without smoothing the edges to avoid risk. A culture where leaders and teammates are willing to take risks if they believe they have created a brilliant, high value solution.

Bees work together, they have a plan, they gather environmental intelligence and resources, and they answer to a leader. Try the hive approach on for size but don't delegate decision making. Don't democratize the outcome so everybody feels good delivering a lukewarm effort. A safe, comfortable consensus groupthink that has a high probability of changing nothing for the better. To achieve excellence risks must be taken. True accountability focuses the team and leader's abilities.

Planning Process Compression

Depending on where you sit in your company's hierarchy, you will often find yourself responsible for designing one plan while simultaneously developing another and executing a third. It's important to take a step back from time to time to evaluate your planning team's capacity to execute more than one planning process. It is very easy to say yes to multiple requirements but easy to dilute effort and attention by spreading people's time and energy across too many imperatives.

As a CEO responsible for strategy and execution across four businesses, I see this play out over and over. Expediency can be achieved without dilution by applying the principle of process compression. This technique is used by the SEALs whenever they have quick mission taskings that do not allow for months or even weeks of detailed planning. The method isn't all that inventive, you just follow the approved quality planning process at high speed, without skipping steps.

I've performed compressed planning drills in every aspect of my personal and professional life so I'm comfortable with the idea, however many people are not. I've performed compressed planning for successful combat missions with as little as an hour to prepare, without skipping a critical planning element. I've participated in solution design and four hundred page proposal build for a multi-million dollar government bid by filling a room with experts and a speed typist. In a sense a stenographer, capturing and then typing the solutions to each element of the requirement as they were conceived. A sort of rapid prototyping approach that completed the project in fourteen hours to meet a key submission deadline. We didn't cut corners and we didn't skip a proposal process step. It can be done.

One key to successful compressed planning is numbers. You need to assemble a lot of your smartest people and assets. They can feed inputs into the plan, together in a room, through conference calls, video conferencing, or all three. This trick may help to accelerate a plan under development to make room for a new planning demand signal. Or it may allow for more solution design time before committing to compressed plan development.

Sequencing Planning Efforts

A good reason to consider compression is planning overload. Too many planning projects of various complexity and impact (read criticality) are all on your plate at the same time. I like to step back and look at all the business efforts and then place each in perspective, rate their value to the company, the truth of their due dates (critical timing or adjustable), and the convergence of demands on scarce resources other than time (choke points defined by the number of available key financial analysts, graphic artists, experts, etc.).

Once I see the projects up on a board or graphically

displayed, I can understand their resource-oriented relationship to each other. Compression can be used to pause one project while accelerating another smaller one, regardless of due dates. In today's rapidly changing operating environment linear production of business solutions is a recipe for disaster. Parallel projects, exchanging resources smoothly while hitting every key phase and milestone, can and do work. Combine this project triage method with compression planning you have a few options to perform multiple planning activities without saying no or getting sloppy.

Your last option for managing this hectic task list is to simply say no. I can tell you that not considering this option is a mistake. If pressured, you can point to your track record of smart planning, successful solution design, and superior project outcomes. Your boss will should understand that saying no, is a smart choice, the alternative may derail the successful approach you've implemented. He or she will appreciate the value of your leadership style and will back off those few times when your plate is truly full.

What Can go Wrong, Will go Wrong

So, now you're perceived as a brilliant, efficient planner and things couldn't go any smoother. I can't finish this chapter without noting the role Murphy's Law can play in planning outcomes. The rule is well-worn, quoted frequently, and applies to everything in life. As a SEAL and as a business leader I knew I could only do what I could do, but fate might have a different plan in mind.

This is true once and awhile for all of us. The tools and techniques covered in this chapter are just as effective if Murphy trips you up. Navy SEALs rely on standard operating procedures when the plan goes awry. They move, shoot, communicate, and create a new plan based on the new reality. Every SEAL knows the planning process and trusts the others know it too, but when the plan goes sideways, they don't abandon intelligent design. They improvise, compress the planning process, then execute.

I've applied these principles of planning to business successfully for over twenty years. A well-trained and motivated team of business planners can recover quickly from adversity and setbacks, apply the standard operating procedures, move, act, communicate, and execute a compressed planning drill to retake the initiative and adapt to the new reality. Trust me, invest in your training, and stick to your process steps and you'll give Murphy a run for his money!

Learn to Thrive in Chaos

SEALs and entrepreneurs are energetic, hopeful, and disciplined. They see opportunity everywhere and are not afraid of the adversity that being in the arena brings. A sense of humor is a prerequisite for a member of the special operations community, and I suggest as a leader you put time and attention into morale while planning. Stress is normal. Fear and depression are not. Do not lead by force derived from positional power but instead, lead through humor, poise, and optimism.

I have survived bad plans where lives were lost and bad plans where businesses were severely impacted. I learned by watching these examples and many more. This chapter has been focused on creative planning, how to look beyond the project management logic of engineering processes to the intangibles, the people and the potential for superior solutions that just might change the world. You can do this. You can relax, be in control, take risks, be accountable, and create great outcomes. I have faith in you. Have faith in yourself and you will succeed!

Chapter Ten

The Black Swan

"When you reach the end of your rope tie a knot and hang on."
Abraham Lincoln

A Black Swan event is characterized by an unexpected death blow or near-death experience suffered by a company, an organization, or even a nation. Several books have examined this phenomenon in recent years, and they agree on two points. First, the data leading up to the Black Swan event was always there for leaders to see; it just didn't match their narrowminded view of their world or market, so the data was ignored. Second, once the event happened, most leaders continued to ignore reality or the new normal created by the event.

According to these studies, only a handful of nations and companies changed, evolved, or adapted quickly enough to reinvent their organizations and survive. Creative, openminded leaders are surprised less often and are poised to act quickly, when dramatic events occur. You can be prepared for a Black Swan, not by perfect business intelligence or by using prophetic abilities. You can prepare by staying humble, open minded, and nimble.

Black Swan Events in History

There are hundreds of Black Swan events in world history. These events are known to us in their entirety because they *are* history. How do we stop the next one? Archduke Ferdinand, heir apparent to the throne of the Austria-Hungarian Empire, was gunned down by a Serbian anarchist on the streets of Sarajevo in June 1914. What followed was a catastrophic, domino-like triggering of mutual defense treaties plunging all of Europe into World War I. Was this preventable? Sure, in hindsight the lunacy of rigid, event triggered defense treaties, national pride, and loyalty to family (many of Europe's leaders were related), set Europe's leaders on a course of action they felt compelled to follow.

The catastrophe that became World War I evolved slowly by our standards of war today, yet the leaders of Europe couldn't or wouldn't halt the programmed movements of armies, positioning of war supplies, and mass recruiting. They were also unwilling to stop or slow the flow of diplomatic threats between belligerents. They never took a moment to project what war between highly industrialized economies might look like and in knowing back away from the brink. So, war came. Unwanted but unchecked. When it was over an estimated forty million people were lost or horribly injured.

Business Black Swan experiences do happen, and they happen to small and midsized companies all the time, we just never hear about them. So, we are left with what is available, lessons learned, often well after the fact, from the histories of large, publicly traded businesses. In other words, we only hear about a fraction of the Black Swan stories and the valuable lessons learned.

Black Swan events such as the Tylenol poisoning crisis of 1986, the Union Carbide gas explosion in Bhopal India in 1984, the Exxon Valdez oil spill in 1989, and the Deep Water Horizon oil spill in 2010 were devastating to both the corporations involved and the people and environments indirectly impacted. There are no doubt thousands of other examples we will never read about, examples where small businesses were wiped out, or a multi-generational company was destroyed. Black Swans don't discriminate based on the size or purpose of a business or an organization.

Lessons Learned

You would think, once exposed, and educated about Black Swan history related to their field of endeavor, that leaders would apply those hard lessons. Sadly, this is rarely the case, remember World War II? Time passes and the lessons of the past fade, even an event as tragic as World War I. Those blind to the failures of history are truly doomed to repeat them.

Leaders usually rise to take control of businesses by performing approved tasks successfully, and perhaps better than their peers. Nobody hands out a medal to those few leaders who continuously shake things up to prepare for adversity. Especially when the threat is something nobody else in your company, your industry, your market, or your profession sees coming. In fact, preventive and proactive thinking is often suppressed. The status quo is good enough, it's the approved reality, the only reality that matters.

This "toe the line" mentality is generational to an extent. Senior leaders are normally older than the rest of the leaders in the company. This adds valuable stability and insight based on experience, but it's this very experience which may blind senior leaders to the possibilities, threats, and opportunities that violate their personal and professional philosophies. Younger people tend to challenge the status quo but have little knowledge or experience to back up their insights so their warnings and ideas die a quiet death while the organization hums merrily along the plotted course, all is well, don't rock the boat.

In 1925, a highly decorated World War I pilot named Billy Mitchell was court martialed by the United States Army and retired from service in disgrace. His crime? Billy Mitchell had the audacity to question America's air defense posture, and he refused to stay quiet after he was busted from General to Colonel and sent to a remote training base in Texas.

Billy Mitchell's concerns and warnings were heretical in 1925. What were some of his wild claims? Billy Mitchell described how Navy ships could be modified by placing a runway on top sufficient to launch and recover planes loaded with bombs. He specifically cited his concern for the remote Pacific home of the U.S. Fleet, Pearl Harbor Hawaii, thinking Japan could exploit ship launched airpower to attack the United States. His well-written warnings to the Chief Staff of the Army regarding this new plane carrier threat (and as a potential offensive opportunity for the U.S. Navy to adopt) was suppressed and eventually so was Billy Mitchell.

Billy Mitchell was ridiculed, shamed, and kicked out of the Army sixteen years before the disastrous attack by Japan on the American Navy base at Pearl Harbor Hawaii. That attack, on December 7, 1941, consisted of waves of ship-launched airplanes, airplanes that destroyed most of the American fleet and killed nearly 3,000 people. During WWII Billy Mitchell was reinstated to the rank of general and a bomber was named in his honor. It was too late for the honoree to see his warnings vindicated and his good name restored. Billy Mitchell who died quietly in 1936, five years before the attack he envisioned.

Billy Mitchell wasn't a young officer without experience or knowledge. He was an insider, an accomplished performer based on the standards of the time. It was his humility (a highly decorated war hero who was willing to see that both he, his pilots, and the Army weren't perfect) and open-minded willingness to test the status quo that marks him as unique, and yet the system wasn't ready for his genius. It instead attacked him and his ideas in order to defend the system. Companies, corporations, and even industries, do this all the time.

If history tends to repeat itself, and history is comprised of human behaviors and decisions, then we, you, are bound to experience more Black Swans, regardless of preparation and regardless of forewarning. The 9/11 commission studied the attacks on New York and the Pentagon by Al Qaeda in 2001 and came to the same conclusion. The commission found that, much like the lead up to Japan's attack in 1942, America had become complacent. We were too proud to consider a small terror cell could strike a strategic blow. Therefore, the agencies tasked with defending America were blind to any threat that didn't fit their approved definition of a threat.

There were plenty of warnings by the field officers of the FBI, but these alerts fell on deaf ears as layers of leaders farther up the hierarchy of reporting oversight, shoved the insights into a file. The input was acknowledged as curious but not consequential. The senior FBI leadership failed to realize that Al Qaeda saw the twin towers as symbolic of America, the great Satan, and had never stopped plotting to destroy that symbol, even after failing to blow up one of the Trade Towers in 1993.

I'm sure someday we will all see the forensic and detailed *historical* analysis of how the Corona virus known as COVID-19, became a worldwide pandemic. We'll sigh as we read how much of the 2020 pandemic and resulting economic chaos could have been prevented or reduced in scale if only the warnings and recommendations for preparedness had been taken seriously.

Many of these warnings will have come from lower level players, people challenging the status quo but without sufficient clout to make enough of a difference. I have lived this process myself and it gave me no joy to say *I told you so*. The lesson you should learn from this chapter is that most people, leaders, and organizations, do not necessarily learn lessons from the past or apply them. Those that do, those that are ready to act, are far too often not empowered to act. How can you be different?

Leading Before and After a Black Swan

Ah, now we can get to the real purpose of this chapter, discussing how you as a leader can break or at least mute the Black Swan paradigm. As you may have gathered by this point in the book, I'm an advocate for humility not paranoia. Being humble could have been the title of this book because I believe so strongly that it is the foundational behavior and mindset that supports nimble and creative leadership.

By definition, a Black Swan cannot be avoided or detected

beforehand. My experience is we often make our own Black Swans and contribute to the likelihood they will occur by our behaviors, our decisions, on a day to day basis. So, let's focus on what you can control, I don't expect you to avoid a meteor strike, an attack from an enemy of the United States, or worldwide pandemics. Let's instead work on what we have the power to influence and maybe we can diffuse a few Black Swans before they ever take flight.

Wellness Test

Would you agree that a person who is healthy, even in great physical shape, might be better able to survive a major flood? The aftermath of a tornado? It's no different if you are the leader of a business. You must have a program of personal and professional development, established as a daily discipline, to be prepared for the unknown. It starts with you the leader. Are you healthy? When was the last time you had a physical? Worked out? Took a vacation to clear your mind? Napoleon lost the epic battle of Waterloo and by doing so he lost France.

Napoleon was a strategic and tactical genius, and the proof was his long history of defeating the armies of Europe. One historical footnote is cause for debate to this day; was Napoleon too ill from undiagnosed stomach cancer to lead the battle effectively? It was undoubtedly the most important battle of his life, yet he may have been physically incapacitated for much of that bloody day. A leader's physical and mental health is the first line of readiness. A Black Swan will turn your world upside down and your personal readiness is critical if you wish to prevail.

Professionally you must study, become a lifelong learner. If you adopt a humble mindset you should have no problem staying hungry for new insights, new information. I've found a well-rounded study program is useful and it represents half of my professional study program. This includes advancements in technology (not employed by my businesses), politics as they affect trends in regulatory environments (again adjacent but not focused on my businesses) and history.

My history study list includes biographies of business, religious, political, and military leaders. I also read a lot about historical trends. Regardless of the subject, historical trends teach me about human nature over time and the way people act and react to different stimuli. The other half of my study is all about the businesses I lead. I read and listen to insights by zooming out to gain context and zooming back in to gain specific knowledge and information. I even learn a new practical skill if it will help me understand something.

In 2018, I took an online medical billing and coding course to help me understand the medical billing company I was starting up. Being prepared for a Black Swan is work, it's extra work for a leader *if* you truly want to be ready for that day. A grizzled old Vietnam veteran SEAL once told a bunch of us young SEALs that you can't suddenly become prepared *when the balloon goes up* (the phrase "the balloon is going up" meant we went to war. Don't ask me why I've never been able to figure it out). He said, "You go into the fight with what you have and what you can do and hope it's enough."

SEALs train fanatically. There is the scheduled training and then there is what every SEAL does on his own time. The old Vietnam veteran was right, you don't ever know when that call will come and when it does, your time to get ready is over. Prepare yourself now. Be as strong mentally, physically, and professionally as you can be so when the day comes you have a fighting chance to survive your Black Swan event.

Your Leadership Team

Depending on the size of your company you may have direct reports who are responsible for leading or supervising key areas of your endeavor. You should evaluate their readiness and work with them to create for them, a personal and professional discipline of physical and mental wellness. A thoughtful professional growth program should also be encouraged. It will do you no good to follow the guidance I have offered only to find your subordinate leaders are not up to the task when your balloon goes up! Take the time to explain why they need to do more to prepare for a Black Swan and get them ready!

If you lead a large and complex organization, you may want to direct your leaders to pass the above instructions to their subordinates, and so on. The stronger the core leadership of your enterprise is, the more resilient it will be when the moment arrives that challenges all your current assumptions. This will also enable you to rapidly reconfigure your company, based on a new strategy for success that addresses the realities of the new normal. A resilient business is more responsive to change and more successful surviving unexpected and adverse events.

The military routinely uses a process referred to as a Red Team. This exercise places leaders or experts in a room with the same information senior military commanders are using to create their operational battle plans. The players are not aware of the approved plan or plans and they are purposely chosen for their open-minded thinking and intellectual honesty.

Often Red Teams find critical flaws or create insightful solutions not contemplated by the assigned planners. You can use this same method to evaluate any aspect of your company. Test the plans, test the infrastructure, find out what you don't know, before a Black Swan alights on your head.

Your Communications Processes

Today, communications tend to follow organizational structures. Like water flowing through terrain, communications protocols, methods, and processes carve deeper and deeper, creating a rut for your leaders and people to naturally follow. Communicating is important during normal operating times but it's critical during, and immediately after Black Swan events. Waiting to test your communications infrastructure and policies until a catastrophic event occurs is crazy. Don't be crazy!

The United States has practiced strategic command and control of our nuclear weapons arsenal since the advent of the Cold War in the late 1950s. Regular, no notice exercises confirm strengths and reveal weaknesses in the communications process used to either contain or direct the use of these powerful weapons systems. As you might imagine, communications technology has changed considerably since the 1950s and the United States has endeavored to keep pace.

What can you do to better prepare your communications ahead of a Black Swan crisis? I suggest you first conduct an honest review of your information technology platforms and communications software. Upgrade if necessary. Look at these supporting tools and consider a disaster scenario, not normal day to day usage. Do you have a list of personal mobile and home numbers for your leaders? Do they have the same for their people? How easy would it be to gather home addresses? After both the 9/11terror attacks and Hurricane Katrina, cell service was either disrupted or nonexistent for hours if not days. You might find door to door contact is all you have left if the power grid fails and the cell system collapses. Don't believe it can happen to you?

In 2005, Hurricane Katrina struck the Gulf coast of the United States creating a Black Swan event for the President and the Governors of multiple states. The country had suffered through hurricanes in the past and we had sufficient resources, leadership, and emergency support to handle the ones from the past, Katrina was different.

I was part of a defense contracting company, a director of a growing business division in the company when Katrina struck. Within hours we were being asked by the Federal Emergency Management Agency (FEMA), to respond to the disaster with anything we could bring; medics, medical supplies, helicopters, fixed wing cargo planes, patrol vehicles and lots of security professionals.

The president of our company called all twenty or so vice presidents, directors, and department managers into a large conference room. He suspended the approved and well-worn organizational structure and process workflows for the purpose of responding to FEMA's request. He said we were all foot soldiers and that we need to rapidly reconfigure the company to deal with the task at hand.

Within thirty minutes we had collectively identified categories of support, assigned leaders to each category, assigned technical specialists to new support roles, and established a new communications plan to the new mission. The communications plan covered media response and messaging, daily status reporting from our deployed teams in the Gulf region, special emergency request processes and channels, and a tactical level communications plan using line of sight radios and satellite radios (cell phones were not an option for over a month after Katrina hit).

We successfully deployed hundreds of vehicles, managed a thousand security professionals, operated heliports, managed fuel depots, and kept public and private property safe. Our people also were credited with saving scores of citizens stranded in New Orleans. While we didn't have applicable communications plans in place for Katrina (responding to natural disasters wasn't what the company did), talk about creativity under fire!

We invented nearly every aspect of the Katrina response and it was a wonderful thing to be a part of. This example shows you how you as a leader can overcome stale or clumsy communications processes and methods through force of will and directed leadership in crisis.

Your Damage Control Processes

The U.S. Navy doesn't want its ships to sink. Unfortunately, that is precisely the aim of the opposing Navy, so procedures are drilled and practiced continuously to save a ship in distress. Collectively these procedures are referred to as damage control. Damage control consists of efficiently sealing off areas of the ship to prevent fires or flooding from spreading, firefighting and fire suppression, and damage repair such as patching holes in the ship created by a collision or an enemy torpedo.

In the Navy, damage control is a way of life, not the main occupation of the officers and sailors. When tragedy strikes a Navy ship everyone is ready to deal with the challenge. Do you have a damage control plan? Have you, or your department, division, or company ever spent a day brainstorming various destructive scenarios with an eye toward improving readiness, upgrading resiliency, and identifying areas that require regular training?

I've found it is useful to run Black Swan workshops from time to time to divert me and my management team from their daily grind of challenges so they take a moment to address the wild cards, the what if situations, and crazy scenarios that might affect us one day. For example, my companies operate in a coastal region prone to seasonal hurricanes. We've created business continuity plans to ensure we can function should a hurricane strike our home base of operations. Try the leader workshop idea and see what you find out about your vulnerability to a Black Swan event, what could it hurt?

A Final Word about Black Swans

I'm an optimist and as such I'm a hopeful, almost cheerful, leader. Considering all the reading I've done regarding disasters, wars, and chaos, I should be depressed about the future, I'm not. My optimism is derived from my understanding that the fight's not over until you quit. I feel a desire and willingness to face up to the struggle, to prepare myself and my team for the worst possibilities we can envision, and to prepare us all for the ones we cannot foresee. I've suffered through divorce as a child, my own divorce as a father, leading men in combat, untold injuries, two bouts with cancer, the loss of my twenty-two year old son, and twenty-five years in business. Yet I'm *still* optimistic. Embrace the guidance in this chapter and I believe you will become and remain a successful and optimistic leader as well!

Chapter Eleven

Strategy and Timing Your Pivot

"Without strategy, execution is aimless. Without execution, strategy is useless."
Morris Chang

The infantry has a basic function in time of war, seize key terrain, dig in, and prepare to hold that terrain until given the order to move forward to the next key objective. Once an infantry unit takes a position, usually by virtue of human sacrifice and expenditure of materials, it would be foolhardy to rush off to the next objective right away unless prepared. The infantry leader arrives on the target, directs his unit to establish a defensive perimeter, and if needed, digs fighting positions.

Once in control of the space, he or she counts heads to ensure all his people arrived at the objective with him. Ammunition is also inventoried and allocated evenly to ensure no one is short. This drill is executed to prepare the infantry unit for a possible enemy counterattack. The leader ensures everyone in hydrated and fed. He establishes a watch rotation schedule so some can sleep while others stay awake and alert. Then he reports his readiness to hold or receive new orders.

The failure to prepare for a competitor's reaction to your success is the reason many successful businesses fail to retain their hard-won gains. A business may grow rapidly, seizing opportunities and market share so quickly they overload the labor structure, burn down cash reserves, and burn out leaders at every level. It's difficult to lead zombies to higher and higher levels of success without stopping to regroup, consolidate resources, and prepare for the next major effort. Winning and growing is exhilarating at one level, but sustain that rapid ascent, and things can begin to fall apart.

This is also true for dramatically restructuring organizations. Too much creative rework can overstimulate and overwhelm people. Many of your people will still be struggling to adapt to your last set of changes when you decide to implement more of them. Scaling and reorganizing to meet increasing demand are prudent but so is a modicum of stability from time to time, a pause in the battle to stabilize things again.

Businesses continually scale, up or down, as leaders compete in their chosen markets. Too much creativity without prudence may lead to collapse. Not enough creativity leads to stagnation and a slow downward spiral to insignificance. This chapter looks at the merits of planning, executing, winning, "digging in," and then launching forward again, intelligently. Be aggressive but be realistic and protect your gains before lurching ahead blindly.

Why Do You Need a Strategy?

Baseball Hall of Fame player and manager, Yogi Berra was fond of commenting about the value of planning. He said, "When you come to a fork in the road, take it!" a quip that sheds humor on the plight of many leaders. So, do you need a plan, a master strategy to guide your efforts? My take is much like Yogi Berra's. I've witnessed military units wander from mission set to mission set, struggling to decide what they should focus on until war broke out when reality suddenly made everything clear. Why all the mission focus confusion prior to the war?

The United States Marine Corps doesn't suffer from this problem. Their ethos, their traditions, and their sense of collective purpose are all wrapped up into one cohesive, yet simple strategy. Any good Marine knows their reason for being, their roles and responsibilities. As a result, the Marines are the best prepared of all the U.S. military services when war does erupt. They don't have a steep learning curve when the bullets start flying and they don't have to pivot from where they were focused during peace time to where we need them when that nasty balloon goes up. As a leader you can emulate the Marines focus by creating a strategy that reflects your vision and your culture, then communicate that to your organization.

I often counsel business owners, leaders, and management of non-profit enterprises on strategy. A strategy is a cardinal direction that takes you from where you are to where you want to go or what you want to be. It is not a short-term operational goal achieved in less than two years. Strategy serves as a beacon, a signpost, a directional marker that keeps you as a leader on track to achieve the big objective.

What is a Strategy?

Often telling someone what a strategy is is harder than conveying what their strategy should look like. Project milestones are not strategic end states, operational objectives are not necessarily strategic in nature, and if your "strategic" goal can be achieved quickly it probably isn't audacious enough to qualify either.

I was mentoring a retired military officer once, a graduate of the U.S. Navy War College and founder of a marginally successful small company. He asked for help in evaluating his business strategy and I happily agreed.

The first question I asked was "so, tell me what your strategic goal is, then we can discuss how you are trying to reach that goal." He nodded and promptly began to tell me, in detail, about his competitive market, the opportunities that existing in that market, and how his sales were doing in the face of stiff competition. I scratched my head, fidgeted, and listened politely. I already knew how this was going to end.

I pointed out that his appreciation of his business strategy was in reality a firm understanding of his market, his sales, and his competition. Operationally speaking his grasp of business development was impressive. The problem was he thought it was strategy. By the time another hour had elapsed I'd was able to apply military examples of tactical, operational, and strategic goals to show him his mistake and to show him he already knew the differences between these three levels of thinking and planning. We ended the session with a homework assignment. After four years in business he did not have an end state in mind for his company or for himself as founder and owner. He was to reflect on this and return when he was ready to layout his strategy for my review and guidance.

This example illustrates what leaders in many small to medium size businesses do. They focus on the day to day grind and look a short distance into the future, again focused on tactical or operational threats and opportunities. For the owner of a successful bicycle shop it is easier to win the gross sales minus costs game than to consider the value of his business, the potential to sell that business, or the possibility his or her brand is strong enough to start another store across town.

A strategy doesn't have to be complicated, remember the Marines? A coherent message describing where the "unit" is heading strategically can fit on one sheet of paper. This is true for the military as well as businesses of all sizes. A strategy defines what is important as an *end goal*. The path or the "how" can also be simplified for ease of comprehension and communication to all levels of your team, group, business, or organization.

Communicating Your Strategy

A single page strategy that communicates the intention of the company, identifies a standard for execution, and provides a timeline or other measure to identify what success looks like, can be boiled down into concise directives. The age of voluminous strategy dissertations, written for external stakeholders, banks, or posterity, is over.

The shelf life of these overly detailed plans in today's hyper paced change is short, rendering moot those lofty thoughts almost as soon as they are printed, bound, and filed. What's more, most leaders and rank and file technical performers rarely get to see these prized documents. If they did, they'd be hard put to understand them. A strategy can be as simple as, "we will all leave Egypt and cross the wilderness until we reach the promised land." Or "we will put a man on the moon by the end of this decade." Direct, simple, and memorable, works.

Communicating strategy is even more important when challenges to that strategy require you and your business to pivot slightly to deal with an unexpected positive or negative situation. Pivot from what? That's right, if your company doesn't understand the current strategic plan, how can they pivot smartly?

Shiny Object Syndrome

In the classic children's book, *Alice's Adventures in Wonderland,* written by Lewis Caroll, the Cheshire Cat assists Alice when she asks for directions by offering "If you don't know where you are going, any road will take you there." Besides not having strategic goals or a path toward those goals, most leaders and employees see opportunity as strategy defined. I've often heard this behavior called shiny object syndrome. The compulsion to react to a new product, or service idea, a new market opportunity, or a new mission statement and consider it so incredibly fortuitous that it (whatever it is) must be pursued at all costs as *strategy*.

We are humans and as such we are emotional creatures. Shiny object projects should not be confused with a strategic pivot. One is emotional and grossly misaligned with the strategy in place, and the other is a slight adjustment of the current strategy. Leaders of small companies, big companies, or divisions within large companies, are all tasked with projecting the future for themselves or for their senior leaders.

Corporate or company strategy writ large, should be a clear

cardinal direction that is communicated from the very top. However, your task may be to create a supporting strategy at your level of accountability. A subset of the greater plan that if achieved, helps the larger organization reach its greater goal. Being strategically misaligned at a subordinate level of leadership happens all the time. One cause for this misalignment is what I have already mentioned, poor crafting and communicating of the overarching company vision.

I had a gifted, intelligent, and energetic executive reporting to me once in a startup focused on healthcare. This executive's focus every day was process management, systems validation, tightening up execution, and limiting labor costs. He achieved this and was proud of his success. As impressive as this was, it wasn't aligned with the strategic intent of creating the startup in the first place. That strategy required the new investment to grow rapidly, seize as much market share as possible, and beat the competition to the punch over a thirty-six-month period of continuously scaling business operations.

In hindsight I must take responsibility for this disconnect, in part because my strategic intent was buried in a tome created for a bank, using the bank's format. It was a complex business plan reflecting a checklist for bank funding rather than a tool that conveyed my strategic intent to my executives and through them to our employees. That was only four years ago, and we learned this lesson the hard way. The startup stumbled and sputtered, falling short of strategic growth expectations while at the same time operating internally like a well-oiled machine. I've since started using a one-page strategy approach. Clear, clean, and memorable.

Time to Pivot?

A strategic pivot is a change in cardinal direction that is minimal yet appropriate. Think of it as trimming the sails when the wind direction changes. You are still heading toward your intended destination but to get there you need to adjust a bit. I've had experience with two strategic pivots in the past twelve years. The first was thrust upon me and my business partner in early 2010.

The major offensive military operations in Iraq and Afghanistan were winding down to a level where the Department of Defense used fewer and fewer contracted assets to make ends meet. We could see that our total business commitment to, and reliance on, the Department of Defense as our sole customer was to become a threat to our existence in the years ahead. The time to identify this and act was two years before this likely shift in federal spending became a real crisis.

Within three years we had continued our impressive growth rate and the Department of Defense represented only one third of our total business. We had pursued a pivot strategy and established significant contracts with multiple federal agencies such as NASA, the Department of Homeland Defense, and the U.S. State Department.

The pivot wasn't about changing our business, we remained a professional services company delivering quality outcomes to the U.S government. We simply adjusted the sails to survive a change in the federal market, a shift in the wind. We pivoted away from our best and only customer and diversified our customer mix.

The second, and more recent strategic pivot happened after that same federal contracting company became an employee owned entity know as an ESOP. It was the spring of 2015, and we had plenty of running room ahead of us. We also had several major contract bids awaiting award decisions. My Chief Financial Officer and I took some time to bask in the glow of recent successes. That was the moment when I decided to red team the potential futures facing our newly formed ESOP. What came out of that series of brainstorming sessions changed everything.

To offset shrinking federal contracting margins, it was clear we needed volume of gross sales to sustain our success in 2015 and beyond. The long anticipated reduction in Department of Defense spending had indeed happened and we were happy we'd successfully pivoted to new federal customers in the three years after 2010.

Now we realized any government contract awards going forward would be highly price competitive. As the shrinking Department of Defense pie got smaller and smaller companies went under. We lost a lot of our competitors, names we'd strategized against for ten years. Big defense companies shed their personal services divisions and turned back to making planes, tanks, and ships.

I determined that to survive and grow the next strategic pivot couldn't be in the federal market. In 2016, after a twelve month search, we bought a small healthcare company. Since that leap of faith, the federal contracting company has shrunk by twenty percent while the healthcare portfolio of companies (yes, we continued to expand this pivot strategy) grew exponentially.

As a CEO of an ESOP my task is to protect, and then grow shareholder value. Staying the course in federal contracting after 2015 would have failed to meet that mandate. The four ESOP operating companies are all professional services based entities and collectively we still protect, and train American military and law enforcement professionals while at the same time providing exceptional medical care to older Americans. The addition of healthcare was a pivot for sure, but not off target from our vision in 2009 to serve and protect Americans around the world. Strategic pivots do not require a change in core competences, just an adjustment regarding who, or how those core capabilities will serve.

Don't be afraid to pivot when the facts drive home the need to do so. Look to the future and accept the changes you see coming. Hiding your head in the sand, hoping the future will go away is foolish, the future always shows up. Ensure you consider pivoting before creating a radically new strategy. Many anticipated changes only require slight corrective judgements. You should reserve radical changes in strategy for when you must cope with Black Swan events that threatens your very survival. In that circumstance, your strategy must allow you to live through the chaos to fight another day.

Over Diversification as a Defense

Small businesses often take years to stabilize and they are always vulnerable to larger chain competitors or the whims of trends and fashion. One thing many small and middle-sized business do to survive is diversify their work. This is different than diversifying your customer base as discussed previously, I mean, your selling hot dogs *and* renting bicycles? Your selling casual shoes *and* trendy books? You get the point. In this paradigm the business doesn't have a strategy, it has a reactive program of day to day opportunities that all satisfies a sort term desire for revenue only.

This form of diversification becomes a comfortable defensive *tactic* that provides owners with multiple revenue streams. Large corporations may also use diversification of products and services through acquisitions to bolster their financial statements. While this method of diversification may be appear to be helping the top line, it can also hide serious problems related to the core business, problems that won't seem as urgent if other revenue is pouring in to mask the underlying challenges.

I only bring this to your attention to ensure you hear from me that diversification of products and services as just described *is not strategic pivoting*. It is the antithesis of strategic thinking and the art of adjusting your well-thought out strategy slightly (pivoting) to deal with unforeseen challenges. Beware of the lure of shiny objects and the promise of revenue through diverse lines of business, you may be surprised in the end that you've weakened the core business.

Value Creation and Exit Planning

My job as the CEO of an ESOP is value creation as measured in dollars per share. This value is reported annually to each employee owner. This responsibility is similar to a CEO of a publicly traded company but without the public scrutiny or daily valuation expressed in the stock market. Over the last few years, I've learned what positively and negatively affects our ESOP's value and as you might expect, it is the same list of value drivers that affect the market value of any company.

Strategy is key here. So is staying the course and fixing problems on the way to your strategic goals. Most buyers or valuation professionals will tell you that a niche business with a strong customer base and solid financial statement is more valuable than a similar company that is widely diversified. This means the market and buyers in the market, don't care about the side business renting bikes, they are looking for pure play purchases to grow their hot dog empire.

It doesn't matter how small or how big you are, this valuation principle is the way the market works. At one point we considered selling our original federal contracting business. We provided our contract customers with two services: training and security. We started with eighty-five interested parties but quickly lost sixty percent of them. The buyers wanted either a training company or a security company, but not both. The sale process ground to a halt and we continue to operate that company within the ESOP today.

I mentioned mentoring a former military officer earlier in this chapter who asked me for help in devising a business strategy. What I failed to note was his total lack of a personal exit plan. An exit plan is a great exercise to help you, if you are either a business owner or in a position to advise one, to create a strategy that not only includes growth and improvement but one that also takes care of the founder or the senior leaders of an enterprise. I'm not saying you have to commit to selling to craft a great strategy, but it does help you focus. Leaders who have an eye on the prize rarely chase shiny objects!

A New Strategy is Born

Then the day arrives! You have achieved what you set out to achieve. If this results in a sale, congratulations. Even if you are not the owner your strategic guidance and vision, your discipline and steadfastness helped make it happen. If a sale isn't in the picture it's time to start all over again. Evaluate the external environment, the competition, how what you do in the market resonates (or doesn't). It's time to create a new game plan supporting a new one-page call to action. Keep it simple, communicate always, and when necessary, pivot!

Chapter Twelve

Two is One and One is None

"The secret of crisis management is not good vs. bad, it's preventing the bad from getting worse."
Andy Gilman

SEALs have many clever sayings, and this chapter is named for one of them. As a leader you are responsible for paying attention to your company's strengths and weakness and understanding the demands of both current and future operations. In the last chapter we discussed strategy development and how leaders can successfully steward their businesses over time to reach a declared strategic outcome. In this chapter we will look at leading through operational challenges, challenges that may be delegated to subordinate leaders, managers, supervisors, or even subcontracted vendors.

Scarcity creates demand externally unless you rely on an external resource to operate your company. Scarcity in this case could be a threat to execution. Internal scarcity in talent, time, money, or adequate technology, can cause you to fail, even when the external market is screaming for your products or services.

Even the best leader armed with a brilliant strategy, incredible offerings, and high demand for those offerings, can fall short on delivery. As you may be gathering by now, leadership is complicated. You can be great in one aspect of the job description but fail in several others. We'll spend some time discussing how to be prepared for success through prudent steps taken before, during, and after a high demand event or business cycle in your world.

When Should You Assess and Prepare?

The military teaches preparedness and situational awareness as a survival skill. Considering the life and death nature of military operations, most service members buy into being ready and knowing what constitutes a threat and where it may be hiding. In general, since my retirement from military service I've not observed organizations follow this policy of prudence and awareness. Maybe it's because most organizations are not concerned with, or exposed to, the consequence of death or injury the way military personnel are when they go about their work.

Life outside the military may not be as high risk, or the consequences of failure so dire, but the principles of readiness and situational awareness are just as applicable in business. Another observation I've made is the general lack of single-minded focus on the group, or the whole. The company. This holistic focus is prerequisite for leaders in military units worldwide.

This observation isn't a dig on those who go to work every day not wearing a military uniform, it's just a behavioral trait of Americans who live in a free society. Americans can focus on themselves. The U.S. Constitution preserves the pursuit of happiness in the Bill of Rights, so it's fine to care more about yourself and your family than the company that pays your wage. This fact of life in America means civilian leaders have a tougher job than military officers and senior enlisted leaders. It makes it more difficult to pull and push the population of a business toward any objective, short term or strategic, low reward or high value reward.

As a leader you should be focused on past, present, and the future. You must assess your ability and capacity to cope with the here and now, colored by recent past lessons learned. Scan every category of your business. Financial resources, labor mix and talent available. Understand if the space you use to execute is sufficient, or excessive. There's more.

A prudent leader isn't afraid and isn't risk adverse. A prudent leader is leaning forward into a future unlived to prepare to seize great opportunity or fend off great threats. Preparing for the future must be a learned behavior, a daily thought process so natural as to be a part of a leader's game plan without making it a separate project. Short range, intermediate range, and long range. Out and back and out again.

Brushing your teeth is preparedness, seeing the dentist is prudent. If you never get a cavity you can say it was all a waste of time and effort or you can smile and say it was worth doing. Preparing for the unknown in business is a lot like brushing your teeth. Make it a part of your daily leadership discipline. A habit with a positive payoff!

Cramming Before the Exam

Getting ready for impending scarcity makes sense and doesn't require much discussion or effort, yet most people, leaders too, fail to get ready for lean times until those lean times are staring them in the face. Nimble leadership is creative leadership so take a few minutes to assess operational level scenarios that may not be probable or even possible but may happen anyway.

I'm pretty sure early man wasn't planning for the Ice Age, it happened to them, nothing personal. The onset of a new age was external to their daily framework of risk and success. In my experience lean times are often imposed upon us by forces outside our control or beyond our view of things and that's why they test us. We get caught short without time to prepare.

This is a law of the universe so why wait or wonder? I spend time gaming out different scenarios for each of the five companies I lead. I look at what we should know and what might happen and then study our readiness. I also look at asymmetrical threats, forces beyond our control that will affect us even if we are doing everything right.

A power grid shuts down, not my fault. Impact? Work around in place…or not? Tariff war, natural disasters, union strikes, and swings in political philosophy and regulatory controls due to elections. Not my fault. What *is* my fault, is being so arrogant, or so blind, that I ignore what I can't control, and pretend the threat I didn't see coming, isn't important.

Evaluate your readiness against all threats, known and unknown. Prepare your leaders and have them prepare their direct reports. Strive to have a collective, companywide mindset that is prepared, and continually preparing, for adverse conditions to arise. If being ready is a component of your culture, Murphy's surprises are just that, surprises, and not emotional or financial shock waves.

Preparing During Boom Times

The feeling during times of plenty is there will be no days of scarcity. It's the same way with success. String multiple wins together and a leader, and their company, can begin to believe it's normal to win, all the time. If the Novel COVID-19 pandemic taught us anything it was that most Americans were not prepared for their food, their paper towel, or their toilet paper supplies to last more than a week at best. Once scarcity was clearly the new normal, hoarding began, and hoarding created even greater scarcity. When times are good it's the best time to prepare for things to change for the worse.

A good leader should be a student of disaster. There is great value in studying the process of bankruptcy. Observing or studying how companies react to crippling natural and unnatural changes of fortune. You will glean many valuable lessons by doing so. You can also play out the sequence of someone else's misery by applying it to your company. Would you have been surprised, unable to handle shortages of labor or material? Would you have allowed yourself to become financially overleveraged during the boom times only to find in an emergency nobody will lend you additional funds so you can survive?

I get no joy in learning from other people's failures but I do glean insights and see that humility is hard when everything is going your way and it is humility that keeps us concerned enough to maintain situational awareness and prepare for the worst, even during the best of times, *especially during the best of times!*

Redundancy Equals Resiliency

Deep bench strength, a brain trust, defense in depth, all relate to establishing and maintaining operational resiliency. Redundancy is easy to create if you have a mind to do so. As noted earlier, it is far less likely leaders will prepare for challenging times while experiencing good times so how do you ensure redundancy and resiliency is in place? In a word, discipline.

Discipline begins with you, the leader, in your personal life and in your day to day actions as an executive. Some of the following suggestions and insights require you and your people to do more than just their job description. They require an additional commitment in time and in some cases, money. They require planning and execution everyday even when there doesn't appear to be any time to spare. In a word, they require commitment.

Redundancy is doubling or tripling up on people able to perform critical skills, key infrastructure capabilities, hardware solutions, software, or cloud-based systems, outside sources of supply, niche partners, and any other vital external support. Resiliency is the outcome of prudence, preparedness, and of course, redundancy in each of your critical operational areas. Let's begin with one of my favorite ways to become, and remain, strong as a business. Cross training.

When Should You Cross Train?

In general, training members of a team, a business unit, or any organizational division of work, improves capabilities, skills, and operational knowledge in each person's core area of expertise. Training improves function and functionality. It strengthens the organization. However, you don't want to stop there.

As a nimble leader you should be thinking about operational challenges in a multi-dimensional manner. You've thought about Black Swans and assessed your risks to wild card events, you've assessed your company's mission and strategic goals and created a roadmap to attain those goals, now you need to apply the discipline associated with a commitment to resiliency. To not do so invites uncertainty and crisis that could have been avoided or greatly minimized.

By now you've probably guessed the answer, you should cross train everybody, all the time. In my experience, a large percentage of your people will enjoy, or at least tolerate the enhanced professional learning opportunity, but there will be those who see it as an uncompensated burden and not embrace cross training happily.

If you start employee indoctrination into the value of cross training from the beginning of their onboarding; your leaders, administrative, and technical personnel will see redundancy and resiliency for what they are, strong defensive (and sometimes offensive in the case of seizing new opportunities), capabilities that make their business stronger and their future's more secure.

Implementing a vigorous cross training program throughout your organization is so important it has become one of my first steps upon being placed in a leadership position. The challenge for leaders is we don't get to onboard everybody the same way, all at once. We can start a cultural emphasis on readiness through cross training, but it will not be enough. We will have to direct the existing population to adhere to the new discipline and that will invariably result in push back, direct and subtle.

Employee and management push back manifests itself at the level of execution, not at the senior leadership level. However, your senior leader's level of engagement is the key to successfully implementing cross training as a cultural norm. There will be some passive aggressive rebels who refuse to assume the extra burden. If you or your subordinate leaders give these few people a pass, their attitude can quickly spread and eventually undermine the culture and protective capabilities you are trying to create. Implement, then trust and verify.

Avoiding Log Jams

Another area, not concerned with people or things, is process. Your critical path processes must be streamlined and evaluated for efficiency and effectiveness on a regular basis. Creating new processes or overhauling existing ones is always a pain for all involved and so it is avoided, even if the approved workflow path is no longer being followed. Enter the "work around."

I can assure you that when you need to defend your company or push the throttle forward to seize a short-term opportunity one of the elements of successful execution will be your processes. Work arounds, like Band-Aids, help offset small problems with the approved process, but if you try to push your company, your people, and your material capabilities at a faster pace with Band-Aids in the mix, you are asking for trouble, and maybe failure.

One technique I've used is to periodically ask to see or access key process flow charts and narratives (policies, procedures, checklists, standards, etc.) before sitting down with people living those processes. I don't tell them I've become informed about with what they are supposed to be doing, instead I ask them to walk me through the steps or phases they are responsible for, from left to right in the process. I listen, I encourage white board use, and I take notes. Then I thank them and go back to my desk to compare and contrast what I've heard against what is approved.

Most often there are very few distortions or work arounds and whatever can't be tallied up as nervousness or difference in language, represents little or no justification for intervention and redesign or retraining. However, occasionally, I'm surprised. In these instances, I work my way left and right in the workflow to determine if the disconnect is considerable, or isolated, then direct a full review and redesign to capture lessons learned, usually reflected in a smarter work around that may become the new approved process. Then we issue a new approved process, then train our leaders and technical employees in the new method.

I suggest you begin with what you determine to be the most critical process in your organization and work down rather than reacting to a symptom. Doing so usually leads to a limited and narrow fix without looking left and right in the process to detect root causes and other downstream ramifications.

When should you start this diagnostic journey? As soon as you take charge and every day after that. People continually find smarter ways to get things done, help them preserve those smart ideas and memorialize them in a new approved process so everyone understands the fix.

Process oriented work stoppages are often referred to as "log jams." Much like a mass of loose, freshly cut timber flowing down a river, if one log swings sideways it can interrupt the flow and cause the entire mass to grind to a halt. Pay close attention to your processes and treat them like a garden. Watch over them, inspect them, and from time to time, pull a few weeds.

Avoiding Choke Points – People

We all love our heroic employees, the ones who never make a mistake, the people we work with who reflect the best attitude and work ethic. We instinctively know we could not function without these special people and often wonder what would happen if they left the company.

I love the type of employee or leader I have described. Who wouldn't? So, why am I concerned? To be nimble, resilient, and ready for what's coming around the corner, you need to build bridges over and canals around these stellar choke points. Yes, choke points. These superstars are a blessing, but they also represent a single point of failure. You need to build a defense with depth. Redundancy and resiliency cannot rest on super stars. You must increase your organization's ability to survive or kick into high gear to attack a new opportunity, by avoiding a situation where critical workflow is swirling around one or two key individuals, waiting to be resolved.

Stress the system and your weak points will let you down. Over reliance on star employees is a weak point. Retain these people, lavish them with rewards, and at the same time reinforce the people all around them for the day the star fades or winks out. Don't let increased volume, velocity, and complexity of workflow expose these choke points for what they are. Prepare now, become stronger.

Avoiding Choke Points – Suppliers

All businesses require outside assistance to accomplish their tasks. Your outside vendor relationships are another source of choke point or single point of failure risk. Key relationships who never let you down until they do. I'm not saying your external stakeholders want you to fail. I'm saying they may not be able to cope with your demands, by quality, quantity, cost, and timing, and that means you need to have a plan B.

Outside support also includes operating capital provided by banks, raw material suppliers, recruiting firms for new employee candidates, specialty skills such as accounting and legal advice, you get the picture. Fill in the rest of the list with factors associated with your business. So, how do you prepare for a vendor failure event?

My advice is to cultivate, evaluate, and get cost proposals from at least two backup vendors in each area you rely on for external support. I'm not speaking of bidding wars or doing this exercise just to drive down your current costs. I'm suggesting you might want to have options in hand that you can quickly activate in case one of your go to relationships falters or fails to support you when you need more than normal service and support.

It's similar to the cross training concept, build bench strength in the same way and when the day comes when you are beginning to surge, and your external partners say no to a request for the first time, you can switch horses or augment your existing vendor with a known and vetted replacement.

Two is One and One is None

In the SEAL teams we use the phrase "two is one, and one is none". It can be applied to headcount or critical equipment. The concept of redundancy in combat units has been around forever, the SEALs didn't come up with this idea, but they do adhere to it religiously. I spent a few years watching enlisted leaders ensure that a SEAL Platoon of fourteen to sixteen men was ready and capable of doing their mission, a mission almost always conducted far from help and resupply. The simple adage works.

You can take this a bit too far. The concept of redundant gear went loopy in the SEAL Teams in the 1990s. We started doubling up on everything without thought to weight or direct mission application. If the mission required each machine gunner to carry three hundred rounds of ammo, add two hundred more and make the riflemen carry another two hundred rounds each. We need four different kinds of tactical radios, bring eight to be sure!

You get the picture. Somehow, we went from being the lean jungle fighters of Vietnam to overloaded pack mules staggering under an amazing amount of equipment, weapons, ammo, and everything else the officer in charge could think of. This escalading madness had to stop.

When conducting practice missions, the powers that be would inspect us to ensure we were complying with the redundancy policy. We were never allowed to leave something behind, that was sacrilege. But in 1990 we went to war in Panama. During a pre-mission rehearsal I watched my men struggle to load into the back of a military transport truck. Each SEAL required two men to assist him.

When we came back from the pre-mission rehearsal, I told my Chief to keep everybody together and remain geared up. We found a weight scale in the Navy doctor's office and I asked my Chief to weigh all sixteen men in my platoon. The results were stunning. Each SEAL was carrying an average of one hundred and twenty pounds of equipment, weapons, and bullets. What makes this more insane was the mission, a lightning raid where speed and stealth were keys to winning, not a multi-day trek through rugged terrain. I wasn't supervised at the time, so I decided to strip my platoon down to an average load of seventy five pounds of mission gear. Now we were lightning fast commandoes again, not mules.

You do not have to go overboard by doubling and tripling the resources available to you. Resources are expensive. My SEALs paid that price in sweat, carrying far too much material in an effort to create too much redundancy. Use your common sense and focus on reinforcing your critical people, tasks, materials and processes and you will be that much better prepared for adversity, or glorious opportunity!

Chapter Thirteen

The Hero Complex

"People who don't take risks generally make about two big mistakes a year. People who do take risks generally make about two mistakes a year."
Peter F. Drucker

It has become a cliché that true heroes are reluctant to take credit for their actions. They claim they were just doing their job, or that anybody would have done the same heroic thing. The rest of us listen, nod, and silently disagree. Heroes come in all shapes and sizes, defying comic book stereotypes. A heroic act can also be missed or overlooked if small, despite the positive impact. We all need heroes but once in a while, heroism can be a problem.

Being nimble is not a heroic deed. In fact, this chapter is all about discouraging you from aspiring to become a hero. Why do I take this position? It's simple, I define heroics differently when it comes to business leadership. There is a downside to acting the part of a hero when leading people and that downside, in practice, can be debilitating or it could prevent you from creating and developing the types of ideas and initiatives found in this book.

Navy SEALs are heroic by nature, that is if heroism is defined as abnormal physical courage and conviction in the face of danger. SEALs don't believe the hype. They believe, you guessed it, they are just doing their job. I know from my experiences that SEALs have an edge few military units have and that makes a huge difference in confidence and certainty as they go into battle. As a unit, SEALs think, plan, and fight as a coordinated team. They don't have one-man missions and won't ever send one man out as a scout.

The minimum size of an operational unit is a two-man pair. This configuration works thirty percent of the time, a four-man fire team or an eight man set of two fire teams can accomplish most mission tasks. SEALs are not looking for heroes when they screen applicants for their programs, and they don't score individual heroics in training as highly sought-after attributes; especially in leaders such as officers. SEALs only work well when the team executes together.

Are there examples of SEALs who became heroes? Of course, there are. If you had the privilege to speak with one, they would explain, almost to a man, that the circumstances that required heroics occurred because the team broke down, due to overwhelming enemy action, poor planning or just dumb luck. They would reiterate if their team had executed all aspects of the mission precisely as planned and envisioned, the adverse conditions would never had materialized, and they would not have been required to do anything extraordinary.

In business, a good plan executed by a strong team, should not require leadership heroics. Building a strong team is one of the critical elements of any leader's job description. It is easier to lead a strong team, and a strong team can handle most, if not all, of the challenges it faces. Let's talk about heroism and leadership and why you should be wary of the inclination in yourself, or your subordinate leaders.

The Junior Officer Paradigm

War movies depict young officers as weak, confused, and generally a burden the enlisted men carry into combat. This isn't necessarily the case, especially in elite military units. What I've observed is different and just as problematic. Young leaders trying to gain the respect of their direct reports not by befriending them or ignoring their mistakes, but by trying to prove they are just as capable operationally and professionally as their men.

Why is this an issue? The answer is both simple and complex. The simple explanation is no young leader is going to know everything, or be able to perform every task, as well as his or her direct reports. Officers have one distinct function, *to lead*. Leadership is not about competition with your subordinate leaders or your team of seasoned experts. This behavior is a manifestation of a leader's lack of confidence and does not demonstrate they are capable of leading well.

In the SEAL teams, I witnessed young officers vigorously compete to win. They wanted to be the quickest runner and swimmer, the best shot with any weapon, and even the best drinker. It took me a few years of maturation before I began to realize this behavior didn't count for much and actually represented weakness. Eventually, I became senior enough to become responsible for the training of young leaders. Trying to get these leaders to realize leadership isn't the same as trying to get a varsity letter in high school was a challenge.

Interestingly, I saw the same paradigm in operation in business when I retired from the service. While most organizations do not have the rigid rules for leadership tenure and advancement found in the military, they do have rules, and these rules are often a problem. The military slows the ascent of a leader down to a pace dictated by tradition and common sense.

Military leadership theory holds that young leaders, given time and mentoring by their bosses and the senior enlisted leadership, will grow eventually into steady, reliable officers. Even though it works to a degree, I hated this system because for lower tier leaders it wasn't based on merit or performance, but on tenure, specifically time served in each progressive rank.

The business world doesn't always reward merit with advancement, but it does happen, thrusting the lucky and the competent up the leadership ladder. Without the time to mature, many business leaders are thrust into positions they aren't ready to handle. A middle ground between pure tenure focus advancement and merit based advancement is probably the best choice.

In the commercial world, the junior officer paradigm tends to manifest itself in leaders younger than thirty-five years old. Youth drives a desire for acceptance and respect. A need to show everybody they are not only good leaders, but great leaders. That is a lot of self-imposed stress and in almost every case, an unreasonable expectation. Unfortunately, leadership requires some modicum of wisdom, wisdom gained through experience and failure. There are no shortcuts.

Nimble leadership requires poise and reflection. It requires leaders to be comfortable with some level of failure on the way to success. It requires training the entire company, so each person knows their job and performs that job in a manner that ensures collective success. If you are happily acting heroic take a breath and reread your job description. Young SEAL officers were there to plan, direct, and lead, not garner applause.

Military leadership for officers is all about using their brains and often a radio instead of a gun. To solve problems while the team executes the plan and when needed, fight side by side with their team. As an old SEAL Senior Chief once told a young officer struggling with this issue, "Sir, when the shit hits the fan who's going to be doing your job if you're face down in the dirt firing your weapon?"

Lighting Fires

Heroic leaders usually fall into two broad categories, true heroes, and arsonists. Setting aside true heroes for the moment, let me explain this second characterization for you. I'm a Lean Six Sigma Master Black Belt, a designation given to those who complete a long process of training and education in quality control, quality assurance, and quality management. It was

Lean Six Sigma and its process driven, causal effect analysis methodology, that revealed to me there were arsonists posing as leaders among us.

Why would I label any leader in such a disparaging manner? Well, I don't mean to imply some leaders are burning things down using real fire. I'm simply saying many leaders are the actual cause of the crisis they eventually jump in to solve. Self-inflicted wounds and injuries to the organization created by leaders who do not know how, or do not care, to build a true organizational team or thoughtful, functioning processes are the cause of many ailments in business.

One example of this arsonist behavior I discovered several years ago actually involved a true military hero. A leader in combat and then again in business after serving his country. He was sharp, driven, and always ready to answer the call when disasters, large and small occurred. After I observed several of these heroic interventions, I asked him why he was experiencing so many. He wasn't sure at first but then chalked it up to the chaotic nature of our business, our customers, and just dumb luck. At first, I accepted that answer and moved on. Then it happened again.

Symptoms that drive intervening actions by leaders can pop up anywhere along the process but most often they are recognized where leaders are looking, the end state of the process, outcome failure. A supply chain process that threatens to miss a delivery deadline must be corrected by a frantic fix. Rental trucks, late night loading of materials, and emergency drivers is the result of this logistical misstep. It works and everyone sighs with relief. The leader who intervened watches the sun come up and knows he or she has led the team through the crisis.

Oddly, most leaders in this position tend to smile and walk away from what just transpired. They don't expect it to happen again and don't consider looking deeper for a root cause. A driver failed to appear at the loading dock on time equals driver is the cause. Admonish the driver and the problem will not reoccur. A Lean Six Sigma approach might reveal the dispatch and scheduling software that sends the drivers their orders for the day has a glitch. If that is the case our hero is only a few days away from once again putting on the superhero costume and saving the day.

Why do many leaders do this? I believe it's a hangover from their early days as leaders, the junior officer syndrome mentioned earlier in this chapter. The old desire to be perceived as a strong leader is served by acting like a strong leader in crisis. Another reason is a lack of training and education in the art of organizational design and development.

And lastly, many leaders do not develop subordinate leaders to holistically evaluate their people, processes, and systems on a regular basis. That means from one end of the process to the other, preferably before crisis strikes. If best practice elements are in place, fewer issues evolve into crisis and if they do, the team has the skills and the tools to fix the issue, without the senior leader leaping to the rescue. Better to proudly observe the team and system you built resolve the issue.

Cause and Effect Analysis

At first glance the body of knowledge comprising Lean Six Sigma is daunting, but I encourage all leaders to give the program a try. Any solid quality assurance program is big on policy and checklists, and well-defined and detailed standards of performance. Six Sigma is taught with all of that in mind and adds a methodology to diagnose processes and systems to find the root cause of failure.

Casual analysis provides you with the tools to investigate thoroughly, starting at the beginning and tracing the progress of product or service delivery or business process effectiveness. In a nutshell, you observe the linear progression of an activity, and study each connection, resource use, and human engagement for efficiency and effectiveness. You document as you go and once finished, you develop corrective action plans to make things right.

Even if you discover the cause of the problem during your walk down the path to an end state, don't stop. Keep going, observe, record, keep investigating until the very end. Not doing so robs you of full process understanding. Running down processes in this manner can be performed proactively. You don't have to wait for a performance glitch to conduct a quality review.

Causal analysis and holistic, proactive evaluation of your processes and systems will force you to come face to face with how things and people interact with workflow at a level of engagement that matters. It provides you with early warning and in doing so, you are given the opportunity to correct or improve performance steps before a failure develops. There is no need for heroics if you embrace this preventive approach. Make this a regular exercise and you will reap the rewards.

A few years back I was observing reoccurring problems with the way finance and accounting processes were operating. I'm definitely not an accounting or finance guy but when I was confused about why our financial processes were failing, I tried asking my inhouse experts but that didn't help explain things. I decided to conduct a process review of all accounting and finance functions, processes, and supporting systems.

I forensically interviewed each finance employee who touched accounts receivable followed by those who touched accounts payable, payroll, general ledgers, and so on. I drew out the steps and procedures (each step or phase loaded with dollars, time or notes identifying critical equipment, systems, and information technology platforms).

As these experts spoke, I documented it all on a white board. I acted like a detective cross examining each employee by plotting human, machine, and human to machine interactions. After running through each specialty area, I brought the individuals in each subset of accounting and finance together to examine the composite sketch I'd created depicting everyone's perception of what was happening.

As you may guess, there was a disagreement in detail among the participants, but the exercise identified subtle flaws in the way accounting and finance was flowing, or not flowing. We found that the information systems were used exclusively by some, but not so much by others who preferred using old school spreadsheets and calculators. In the end, my facilitation helped my senior finance leaders tighten things up, leverage the expensive information system platforms we were paying for, and helped to evaluate wasteful practices and inefficiencies.

The Price of Trust

In an earlier chapter we looked at the problems associated with perfection and the pursuit of perfection. I've found that people working as a team to complete repetitive tasks, never have the time to achieve perfection or even the inclination to do so. This is where leaders focused on perfection step in. After failing to motivate, cajole, and pressure employees to care about perfection, they step in and try to make it happen all by themselves. A form of leader heroics that is doomed to failure.

To relieve yourself of the burden of perfection and heroic obligation you simply need to trust those doing the work. You must allow your well-designed company, systems, processes, and communication feedback loop to inform you of how things are progressing. A Lean Six Sigma diagnostic evaluation of critical processes and systems, key employees, and subordinate leaders will keep you plenty busy and be preventative in nature, reducing the need for heroic intervention. Trust but verify through quality assurance oversight.

I still have difficulty watching my leaders struggle and

by extension, their employees. I feel my frustration rising, frustration that can only be assuaged by my personal intervention, then I exhale and walk away. Sure, in most cases I could have stepped in and bridged the talent or knowledge gap, but in doing so I make my team weaker not stronger. I feel personally satisfied but over time my leaders and employees will stop trying to figure it out. They will fall into the habit of asking the boss to look at the problem and that is so much easier. What's the downside if he or she screws it all up? Not much if you have your fingerprints on the solution too.

So, I ask you to walk away. Is this advice tantamount to abandoning your sacred duty to lead? Of course not. I didn't say forget about the scenario you witnessed, maybe a process review is in order? Let that meticulous evaluation of the associated processes drive the right leader or technical expert to discover the root cause of the problem and in so doing, your organization becomes stronger.

Trust can be gut wrenching, especially if you've been placed in the spotlight by your boss. Maybe the most heroic thing you can do is to face your fear of failure and your urge to over manage. Instead force yourself to relax. There's no way you can be nimble and creative unless you relax.

When Opportunity Meets Preparation

More than a century ago, Louis Pasteur, French scientist, and the man who invented the process of pasteurization, said "Chance only favors the prepared mind." I've used this quote as a guiding light for over thirty years. During my lifetime I've done, or attempted to do, many things. My personal and professional study habits were driven by paranoia at first. The fear of falling behind, or appearing incompetent to my superiors, peers, and direct reports.

Then a strange thing began to happen. It was as if the universe was guiding me, placing me in the right place at the right time, even if that place had nothing to do with my chosen career or profession. Books on history, especially military history and military leaders had nothing directly to do with my navy job when I was in my late teens and early twenties. Yet all that stored information, insight, and inspiration was there when I decided to become a naval officer at the age of twenty-nine.

Later in my forties I decided to go back and review basic business concepts and methods by creating a reading list that covered all the topics addressed in my undergraduate and graduate work. I made sure I only read state of the art, current thoughts, theories, and best practices. I was a counter-terrorism advisor and asymmetrical threat consultant at the time.

It was post 9-11 and I had no rational reason to study business and no goal to become a businessman. Two years later I found myself in charge of a $40 million dollar a year business division struggling to survive. My wife was the one to point out how weird it was that everything I'd casually read in my days as a threat consultant was vital now that I was leading change management in a large company.

True Heroism and Leading in Crisis

How does this tie into our discussion of heroic leadership? Simple, if you are prepared physically, mentally, and professionally you will lean on that heavily when the day comes, and it will come, when it's time to be heroic for the right reasons. A potential collapse of your business related to the loss of one or more key players can do it. External Black Swan events can legitimately require you to become a hero.

A Vietnam veteran SEAL noticed I was admiring the chest full of medals dangling from the uniforms of several SEALs near me during an inspection. I was too young to have fought in the Vietnam war. I had three medals; not one was for combat action. The men standing all around me were festooned with bright military bling. A Medal of Honor here, multiple Navy Crosses over there, and lots of Silver Stars and Bronze Stars everywhere. They represented the top awards given to America's warriors for extreme valor. In my mind, these men were true heroes.

This older and wiser SEAL told me that SEALs in Vietnam were supposed to be like ninjas, never caught and never seen by the enemy. He then explained that you can't get a Purple Heart or a valor award as a SEAL unless something failed, something went terribly wrong. He believed that, in many ways, SEALs of that era saw these national tokens of respect as symbols of mission failure. I was too young to understand then, but I do now. As a leader your job isn't to be heroic until it's time to be heroic. Think about it. Your mission is to lead and lead creatively. Your day will come and like those Vietnam era SEALs you will realize true heroic leadership is required when everything is falling apart. Not fun.

Chapter Fourteen

Crisis Reveals Character

"When written in Chinese the word crisis is composed of two characters. One represents danger and the other represents opportunity."
President John F. Kennedy

Hollywood has conditioned all of us to believe leaders must be courageous and poised under fire. However, most leaders never face a true life or death scenario and believe me, that's a good thing. Your company is made up people and people routinely turn to their leaders to act in crisis, large and small. When the situation has clearly eliminated the fail safes you have in place, when the odds are against you and the cost of failure is significant, all eyes will be on you, the leader.

This chapter isn't about the downside of heroic leadership, we've explored that topic together already. This chapter is about what happens to leaders under duress, how they cope, and how they can thrive. People do expect direction, guidance, and insight from leaders when things turn upside down. This is patently unfair if the crisis at hand is unexpected, but it's still true.

You are a leader and a person too. You have feelings and emotions. In crisis, your fight or flight impulses will be screaming, interfering with your judgement and in many cases causing tunnel vision instead of objective observation and decisive action. Of course, it's challenging (but manageable) to handle anticipated problems on a daily basis. This might even lull a leader into a comfortable rhythm of normalcy.

The Nature of Crisis

A crisis, I mean a genuine crisis, feels different. It represents not only perceived difficulty but intense difficulty. Your instincts honed by the genetic drive to survive will see true crisis as dangerous. Your job may be at risk, even your career. Your reputation and your self-esteem are also at significant risk in a crisis. Many leaders succumb to a feeling of fear and loss of control when the shit hits the fan and everybody's head swivels around to stare at their leader. This is your time to step up and shine, not shrivel.

Back in the 1990s, a good friend of mine in the SEAL teams was critiquing my subordinate officer, a Lieutenant Junior Grade or LTJG, we'll call Pete for the purpose of this story. Pete was struggling as a SEAL officer, specifically when he made tactical decisions in a fire fight. Now these were simulated fire fights conducted in training with blank ammunition and that made his reactions to this simulated stress even more concerning. Nobody was going to die.

Pete took half of my sixteen-man SEAL platoon out each night for several nights in a row to practice combat patrolling and tactical maneuvers such as breaking contact and escaping once engaged by an enemy unit. I did not participate or observe the warmup drills, but I was the architect of the training Pete was experiencing. I had a highly experienced platoon and Pete's behaviors were causing him to lose the respect of his men.

On the fourth night of training I asked the instructors to set up several ambushes and to get more aggressive with their attacks. Practice was over. By this time, his squad had leaked their disdain for Pete's rigid thinking and particularly, his refusal to take advice from an enlisted man. Now it was showtime, even the commanding officer and executive officer were aware of the problems Pete was having. He needed to succeed or his time in the SEALs would be short lived.

When the fourth night of training concluded, the participants and the instructors gathered to review Pete's performance. It was two in the morning and I was surprised to see our executive officer show up to hear the verdict. SEAL after action critique sessions can be brutal but that's because everyone wants to win, and that means everyone wants to pound out any issues in training, not when under enemy fire. Candor is a must if you are to grow and evolve as a special operator.

Unfortunately, Pete had failed miserably. Ignoring warnings and sage advice from his enlisted SEALs, Pete had stumbled and bumbled for three nights in a row. Then in the last night of the exercise series he walked straight into an ambush. What made it worse was Pete's reaction to the attack. In a panic he shouted out three conflicting orders, and in the pitch-black night his squad split up and moved in three different directions.

It took an hour for the separated SEALs to find each other. Pete's take on the ambush and the entire fours days for that matter, was that he'd been a victim of tricks and traps contrived by the instructors to ensure he failed. Once he'd reassembled his squad in the dark, he unilaterally decided the training was over and directed his men to walk down the beach in plain sight, to the parking lot where the instructors were monitoring their radios. After Pete's rebuttal one of the combat veteran SEALs began to respond.

The SEAL's name was Larry and we had been friends since basic SEAL training thirteen years earlier. Larry was a former Marine who left that service to become a SEAL. We were still close, and I admired his knack for candidly getting to the point. Larry had watched Pete tap dance around his personal accountability for the actions he'd taken during the training exercise until he couldn't take anymore.

He raised his hand, stopping the young officer in mid-sentence. Once all eyes were on him, Larry began to speak. He explained that he'd never had much use for officers in the Marines or in the SEAL teams. They were always the dumbest person in the room compared to the highly qualified enlisted specialists. An unwanted curse and burden.

Larry had everyone's attention. He began to describe his first combat experience during the invasion of the Caribbean island of Grenada in the 1980s. His group of twenty SEALs were pinned down in the open and taking effective machinegun fire from a Cuban armored vehicle. The big gun on top of the vehicle was stitching the ground all around the SEALs and men were getting hit. It was what SEALs refer to as a *shit show*. Then Larry got to the punch line.

As the situation became dire, and most of the SEALs became wounded, Larry said he turned his head to the right and looked at the officer in charge, lying twenty feet away. It was at that moment he realized what officers were for and that most of the other enlisted SEALs were also staring at their leader. This was it. Officer time. Make a smart call! Fortunately, moments later, their officer was able to snap out of his tunnel vison, see a way out of the kill zone, and lead his men to safety.

Larry ended his story with an admonishment. Pete had a choice to make. Be a leader and deal with the crisis and uncertainty combat represented or get out of the SEAL teams. The room was deathly quiet as everyone waited for Pete's reaction. Pete stood there for a few seconds, lowered his head and then nodded. He finally understood his role.

Why did Pete act the way he did when under stress? I have no clear idea, I'm not a psychologist. I have, however, lived through a lot of stress and I feel comfortable giving you my opinion based on observations made at the time and since that night. Pete, and other young officers like him, want to succeed so much they eliminate all perceived risks to that success, that includes help from others which requires trust.

Pete couldn't allow his men to do their jobs, to advise him based on their assigned duty and expertise. That would have required letting go of his fear of failure and trusting in men he didn't know well, to succeed. Pete wasn't going to take that chance. He only trusted himself and so failed as a result of his fears, even while surrounded by eighty years of SEAL enlisted experience that night.

I ran into Pete years later. He was a Navy Captain leading SEALs in the Middle East. Pete had evolved into a solid leader and it was apparent to me that Larry's admonishment, backed by the story in Grenada, had changed the trajectory of Pete's career. Crisis and stress can reveal insecurities. Recognize your negative behaviors when fear drives your emotions and your behavior then work to change those negative behaviors into positive ones.

When crisis strikes, take a deep breath and open your eyes and ears to the information flowing all around you. Relax your grip, even when your emotions are telling you to seize total control. Leverage all your resources. Focus, absorb, analyze, decide, and repeat. Pete changed that night and he never again allowed a crisis or fear of failure shape his leadership behavior.

Personal Readiness to do Battle

As a leader, your personal readiness to enter the fray and lead once crisis strikes is vital to a successful outcome. Being poised, meditative, and always present, takes stamina, both mental and physical. Picture yourself on a small plane with ten of your direct reports. The plane crashes in the mountains and while all survive you are hundreds of miles from assistance. Are you mentally and physically in condition to lead them to safety?

A leader who had envisioned the possibility of disaster, who prepared for it by staging emergency supplies, a solar radio, and a handheld GPS navigation tool, in the plane, would have greatly improved his team's chance of survival. If that same leader had taken classes in wilderness survival, studied plane crash survivor stories, and maintained himself or herself in good physical shape aligned with a wilderness plane crash, leading through the crisis caused by the crash would be far easier.

What does your plane crash look like? Envision scenarios,

write down the sequential storyboard of the event and step back to appraise your work. If the scenario is feasible and the progression of your crisis narrative is rational, how can you prepare yourself? It is the job of a manager to manage things and people through systems and processes. It is your job as a leader to lead when systems, processes, and people fail to cope with crisis. I think you see my point, be ready!

Situational Awareness

We discussed Black Swans earlier in this book and how to prepare yourself and your team for these random, adverse events. A Black Swan is certainly a crisis if we agree that crisis can be defined as a short, intermediate period of time when danger of loss, material wealth, financial standing, relationships, or loss of life occurs. But unlike a Black Swan, a leader may see crisis coming, and be aware of what is unfolding. That form of crisis represents a known risk and because it is knowable, is not a Black Swan.

It is the knowing, the ability to see the crisis coming that makes most crisis avoidable or at least, manageable. The history of warfare is replete with examples of nations, aware of rising tensions, who prepare for the inevitable conflict, or do not. Time is on your side if you create a mindset and discipline that scans the potential or probable risks the future holds, from the horizon of your understanding back to the present.

You shouldn't stop with a forward looking scan. Look back in time and search for indicators of organizational or market oriented environmental stress that portends future failure. Have you detected risk factors hovering just under the surface? These simmering issues seem too insignificant, but they are the seeds of crisis waiting to spout. Maintain vigilance by zooming out, then zooming in, back to the present, then look farther back. Project how small issues may grow into real problems and nip crisis in the bud by acting early!

Planning and Preparation

Crisis leadership sounds like an in the moment activity. It is to some extent, but if you took my thoughts and observations about leadership heroics to heart, you'll agree that waiting for the crisis to happen is just dumb. In a small rapidly growing company crisis is a way of life making leadership an exhausting endeavor. If you are a leader of a small enterprise you don't have a choice, you must be proactive to forestall that adverse effects of crisis. If you don't, the small enterprise will fail.

I'm currently a CEO, a lofty position you may think, one that might be above the blood and gore of daily operational battle. Not so for me, and not so for most of the top leaders of successful companies. There are vastly greater numbers of small to medium sized business, for profit, non-profit, associations, clubs, and other focused groups, that form the lifeblood of America.

Hollywood tends to focus on the big dramatic situations found in large corporations. They love to portray powerful, larger than life heroes and villains in their work. The deals and the steals are big, big, big. The reality isn't anything like what tinsel town portrays. Every day, regular folks, small business leaders, show up to work and resume the thankless job of leading crazy. Yes, crazy. For these leaders, crisis is served for lunch Monday through Friday.

We can all take a few tips from the way the federal and state governments prepare for disasters. They identify critical consumables, materials, and equipment. They also identify services that will be needed during a disaster. Medical, communications, transport, and a whole host of other needs. Once identified they purchase and stage a surplus of important items that fulfill a list created by emergency response planners based on what the disaster scenario is that they've gamed out. It's called disaster preparedness for a good reason and it works.

Do you have a crisis gamed out? How about a disaster such

as a critical supply chain disruption? The sudden departure of a key employee? A service or product failure with potential legal ramifications? These days all organizations have human resource challenges. Preventive action and preparedness in this human capital category can reduce the number of incidents and ensure an incident isn't mishandled once it occurs.

Organizational Mindset

Going back to our plane crash site for a moment, what if you as the leader of the team was physically and mentally prepared to get your people out of the mountains and to safety, but your team wasn't up to the challenge? When crisis strikes an important component of organizational survival is a collective positive mindset and specialized training for the unexpected. That way, when the unexpected happens, people know what the leader will do and what they will be asked to do.

Once you have your crisis scenarios thought out, storyboarded, and you have a plan of intended action, at least your initial actions for each crisis scenario, it's time to tell the troops. Discuss your material and individual preparedness plans and assign people to each area of preparation. This will stick in the minds of your team, readiness and preparation are impactful emotionally. Do this and your business is halfway to a positive crisis response mindset already!

Next, run each scenario narrative by your leaders followed by your leaders running the narratives past their teams. Look for insights and suggestions, apply them, make your people a part of strengthening the company. Do you prepare in this manner now? Have you ever been a part of a business that prepares in this way?

Being a nimble and creative leader means being engaged in evaluating internal and external threats, short term, and long-term opportunities, and staying ahead of life's learning curve. I'm all for a thorough debrief after crisis strikes but if you and your team wasn't prepared why wait for a failure to occur to reveal your inability to anticipate disaster? Learn now, act now, prepare your people now!

When Crisis Strikes

Okay, it's time. You've prepared yourself and your organization. Critical issues are shored up, backed up, and emergency supplies and materials are staged. You've built a resilient operational structure of systems and processes and your skill and knowledge workers have redundancy, others on the team trained to assist or step in and take over as needed in an emergency. Then it happens. All eyes are on you, how do you behave?

Every military person wonders if they will be up to the task assigned to them when it is time to go into combat. Thankfully, of the millions trained for war, only a small percentage see live and direct combat. This means most wonder about their potential behavior for the rest of their lives. Elite forces have a higher probability of seeing the chaos and disruption of war. Repetitious missions and combat tours of duty make them humble.

Combat veterans focus more on the probability of mistakes or accidents happening without warning. A helicopter crash is one example. As veterans, they are secure in the knowledge they are good at what they do and are not afraid to perform their job when the time comes. You might be wondering how you will do when the moment comes. Will you panic? Will you alienate your team by becoming an emotional dictator?

While business crisis in America never rises to the level of bloody combat, we still expect our leaders, and each other, to step up when it's time to dig in and fight back. I've been in both combat and in business crisis. The 2000 NASDAQ crash when I was a money manager was certainly a crisis. It was a shock, sudden and devastating to many stock portfolios over the entire country. My clients looked to me for guidance, even hope. There were about six hundred of them at the time and I wasn't prepared ahead of that economic event.

With only four years' experience as a financial guy, I took a deep breath, pulled up the client list of contact numbers on my computer and began dialing. I kept right on dialing for several days until I had spoken with every one of my clients. Some discussions were better than others but in almost every case I was thanked for reaching out to them proactively to review their holdings and discuss any possible adverse impact of the NASDAQ crash. I learned two important lessons from that experience.

The first lesson I learned in 2000, was that I was one of the rare financial people reaching out to their clients during the NASDAQ crash. Most of my peers and competitors sat back in their offices and waited for the panicked client calls. My unique behavior garnered me a slew of referrals and a ten percent bump in clients over the next few months. Word had spread that I was attentive, empathetic, and intelligent in the face of financial disaster. I found out later that some financial professionals were so shocked and dismayed they hid away from their offices or refused to answer their client's calls.

The second lesson I learned was that I had actually prepared for the crisis with a handful of high net worth individuals. These few accounts had asked for detailed financial and investment plans and programs. Solutions that were customized to their situation and their long term investment horizon.

The conversations with these clients were easy. They told me it was okay, we have a plan, you built it for us, and we have trust in you and that plan. I decided then and there to create investment plans for all my clients, regardless of account size. I evolved after the 2000 NASDAQ crisis, from a sales focused, stock picking guy, to a financial and estate planner who anticipated risk and potential crisis in the economy.

When the shit hits the fan, relax, take a deep breath, review all you have in readiness. Look the part, smile, be firm but comfortable. Your people will watch everything you do and say and take their cues from your projected confidence or lack thereof. If you haven't prepared for a particular crisis get everybody in a room and conduct this speed drill. What is the situation? Cause related to effect (symptom being reported or witnessed)? Lay out the timeline to date and extend it as a projected hypothetical. Draw out the hypothetical timeline as a story board. Stop, assess each phase in your storyboard, identify the most time critical tasks or actions and then assign and launch your team to make good things happen. Reassess and repeat until the crisis is past. Look the part, stay flexible and stay cheerful. You are their leader, act like one!

After Crisis Strikes

It's finally over. You've succeeded, well mostly, and your company will live to fight another day. Now is the time, while the crisis is fresh in your memory, to jot down your impressions. Start with a self-inventory of your performance. Include your readiness before and during the crisis. Then do the same for your subordinate leaders and then their key people. Note who was vital during the crisis and who had challenges. Put the notes away for a few days then pull them out and begin preparing for the next time crisis strikes. If you comported yourself well, congratulations! If not work on the things you need to correct and do it quickly. We rarely choose the moment we will be tested.

Chapter Fifteen

Crowdsource Insights Not Decisions

> *"You know, it's easy for the Monday morning quarterback to say what the coach should have done, after the game is over, but when the decision is up before you, the decision has to be made."*
> **President Harry S. Truman**

I'll give you the headline straight from the beginning. I believe leaders who are granted authorities to act and accepted the paycheck, have also accepted they are responsible for making leadership decisions. Let me be clear, I said *leadership decisions*. Most decisions that are made every day in organizations are not leadership oriented. They fall into job-task functions, and while turning a knob left or right might have dire consequences if done incorrectly, it isn't the category of decision making this chapter is about.

Decisions made one step above functional tasks also do not align with the purpose of this chapter. Many lower level supervisory or management calls are made in accordance with approved policies, procedures, and processes. All of which are usually signed off on by a senior leader accountable for the entire enterprise. Maybe an easier way to dial into to what I'm about to cover is to focus on decisions made by leaders, not managers.

Remember, managers keep approved activities on track. They normally do not invent new policies or innovate in response to a large-scale challenge. We are focusing on the authorized top dog in the pound. Numero uno. If that's you or you want to be that person, read on.

I've participated in many lively debates regarding this topic over the last few years as younger university-trained professionals enter the workforce trained to expect near parity in decision making authority. In some instances, these younger employees have experienced situations in other companies where accountable leaders turn over their responsibility to a group for adjudication and, yes, a final decision.

I try, as a rule, to stay objective and study views contrary to my own. I speak with people who don't share my opinions and I listen to experts that are suggesting things I don't agree with, but why abdicate your responsibility to decide? I hope by now you have a few responses to that question after reading this far in the book.

We started our journey together talking about humility and the power staying humble provides you as a leader. It's this philosophy that drives me to seek out new knowledge and contrary views. So, why aren't I a fan of inclusive, socialized, equitable, and democratized decision making? It's a matter of context.

I think collaborative engagement works wonderfully in design work, the arts, and other areas of the marketplace where creatives merge ideas. However, in professions and industries where compromising or consensus decision making leads to a watering down of performance excellence, simply to comfort the collaboration participants, makes no sense. This social exercise in business can lead to an expensive adverse outcome, loss of competitive advantage, or worse a catastrophe.

As a SEAL officer I sought inputs and insights from my men, the supporting cast of military and government experts, from anyone who could help me, and my team succeed. But when the moment came to decide, I, by virtue of my title, duty assignment, and appointed authority, was accountable to make the call. Right or wrong, there wasn't time to hold a frogman focus group.

So just in case these last few paragraphs have left you thinking I'm a caveman unwilling to adapt to the new methods of thinking, I ask for your patience. At the end of this chapter I'll show you a hybrid approach that can glean the best insights from the best people and sources while not delegating or worse, abdicating the leadership responsibility that is yours alone.

Leadership Accountability, the Navy Way

In August 2017, the guided missile destroyer the USS John S. McCain, collided with a merchant ship near Singapore in the western Pacific. The ship was heavily damaged, and lives were lost. There would be a lengthy investigation to gather the details of the tragic mishap but before those conclusions were reached, the captain, and executive officer of the USS McCain were fired.

This would not stand in most non-military organizations. Leaders would expect a process, findings, and a day in "court" to defend their actions. Later there might be early retirements with high dollar, golden parachutes, or quiet resignations. New leaders would seamlessly arrive and continue the all-important task of leading the organization forward. In the Navy, the first thing they do is fire the accountable leader.

The Navy's view of leadership at the top is based on an earlier period when ships did not have GPS navigation and satellite communications. It was a time when many naval vessels roamed the world independently. Their Captains acted as diplomats, trade representatives, intelligence officers, and from time to time, enforcers. To understand this concept, I encourage you to watch the 1966 Steve McQueen movie, *The Sand Pebbles*. It depicts the adventures of the USS San Pablo in 1926, embroiled in the civil war raging between the waning Nationalist Chinese Government and the ascending communist movement led by Mao Zedong.

The ship's captain, played by the actor Richard Crenna, is operating from a vague mission statement. As the movie comes to a close the captain's sense of mission is at odds with his crew's desire to live. They confront the captain, defying his orders to go ashore.

Led by the upstart but experienced sailor, Steve McQueen, they demand a vote to stay onboard and leave China. The captain listens to their request and denies it, there wasn't going to be a vote. The crew follows their captain ashore and rescues two American missionaries trapped in the turmoil of civil war but the captain and most of his crew do not survive the rescue. Ironically, the ringleader of democratic dissent, Steve McQueen, stays behind and dies fighting so that his shipmates and the two Americans can escape.

My dad was a navy man and we watched that movie together when I was young. I didn't understand why the captain refused the vote or why in the end the rabble rouser sacrificed his life for the mission. My dad tried his best to explain using navy logic, but I remained confused, that is until fifteen years later when I was leading men in combat.

I can see the advantages of the navy's tradition of holding a ship's captain one hundred percent accountable for actions on the high seas. It works for the Navy. I'm skeptical such draconian policies are needed outside of the military but their focus on leadership accountability has shaped my personal leadership philosophy and over the years, out of uniform, when asked who is responsible, I can't say anything other than, "*I am* the accountable leader."

Democratizing Decisions

Socializing a challenge, or an idea, or even a solution, among qualified people in, and outside, of your company in prudent and helpful. I've begun to believe the business schools confused this concept with tossing a group in a room to vote as a new age decision making process.

If you've picked up anything so far in this chapter, sharing the accountability of the outcome voted on by the crew, the gang, the team, etc. actually eliminates all accountability.

That is unless the group has been informed that their failure will result in them all being terminated. Delegating power and accountability to lead or decide is a useless exercise in faux equity. Someone once noted, you will all have a voice, but not a vote. I really like that sentiment.

One problem with democratizing a decision is that, outside of the creative industries noted earlier, most people in a department or a division are not professional peers. They are human beings. Some are shy, others are forceful to the point of bullying. The knowledge and skills are not aligned for each person to be holistically equal as a professional. So, a collective decision, agreed upon in this context, could be comfortable but misguided and dead wrong.

Picture a medical clinic that focuses on brain surgery. A patient arrives complaining of a headache. An Xray confirms he has a tumor that could be life threatening. An intercom message asks all employees to report to the lunchroom where technicians, drivers, receptionists, maintenance, and cleaning personnel all stand along with the physicians and medical personnel training to plan the upcoming brain surgery.

Two of the people in the room are articulate and persuasively voice their opinions. They are not physicians but are well liked and do a great job in the hospital cafeteria making meals. The lead brain surgeon is polite and introverted. He whispers the path he thinks they should take, a path based on experience, training, and skill as a surgeon. Only a few people in the room understand the terms he is using so they become frustrated. The group debates for two hours until interrupted with the news the patient has slipped into a coma. It's time to decide.

That might seem like a silly illustration, but I can substitute brain surgery with corporate strategy, or legal strategy. I prefer to pull together an equally qualified team of people to collaborate, not for inclusion sake, but to gain valuable insights and to produce viable options for me to consider before making a final decision.

The Compromise Decision

An army squad is tasked to take a nearby hill held by the enemy. The young officer canvasses his squad for ideas. Half of his men do not want to attack, and the other half want to take the hill. The young officer makes his decision and takes his squad halfway to the objective and stops. He's honored the opinions of his men and compromised by meeting both sides halfway. The hill does not get taken and his men are ripped apart by enemy fire as they stand together at the halfway point.

That would be a hell of a way to lead people in combat. The analogy applies in business too. Allowing compromise to make important decisions dilutes quality and a shot at true excellence. Compromise is different than bargaining. In bargaining the parties have a choice to walk away if a deal cannot be struck. Two supervisors agreeing to use a limited technology resource by alternating days would be an example of bargaining. Strive to make a decision that works for all concerned and if that is impossible look to the health and strategy of the company to guide you, but then decide.

Dictatorships

Firm, decisive leaders are frequently called dictators by internal observers. In truth, the context of the business at hand is critical in determining if a leader is indeed acting tyrannical. Does he or she ignore all input from subordinates and peers? Do they rush forward blindly applying only their opinion of what must be done, without moderation?

In the example of the squad ordered to charge the hill, the senior officer who gave the order and the young officer tasked with carrying out the order, could both be construed to be dictators. However, the context of the military, its training, tradition, and mission contradicts this labelling. Following orders in a life of death situation saves lives and accomplishes military objectives.

I've found there were a few times when I had to make the call without input and insight from others and that was the crux of the problem, I wasn't receiving any insight or input, only passionate speeches without a commitment to a position or a long speech about the future without recommendations. As noted in the military example, I was usually under a strict timeline and a decision was required in short order. This isn't the preferred way to lead all the time and it is the perception of you as a dictator that is the real risk here. Do it once or twice a year in the proper context and no one will bat an eye. Do it every day and guess what, you're a dictator.

The Consensus Decision

In compromise, the parties are representing their goals and requirements. In consensus, the parties are honestly striving to come to an accord to make the business better, stronger. Consensus is collective judgement best arrived at when people qualified to make the recommendation for a path forward, are experts in the topic at hand. Consensus among wheat farmers regarding how to conduct brain surgery on our patient, in the earlier analogy, may generate a consensus recommendation but should we operate based on that opinion?

Crowdsourcing Insight Internally

Crowdsourcing is a recent term du jour, describing the use of all source inputs, usually through access to social media platforms and the internet, to broaden access to information, ideas, and assistance. I like the term because it goes beyond networking, a methodology that limits you to the size and construct of your network.

While crowdsourcing is usually about gaining access to an external resource or resources, you can use the concept internally to gain access to knowledge, opinions, and ideas, normally stove piped and aligned with the organizational chart and hidden from view. A corporate town hall meeting, physical or virtual, is an example of internal crowdsourcing, off sight planning retreats involving a wide range of internal leaders and technical experts is another.

I've also found that walking around and asking open ended questions is a great way to gain access to this hidden under current of feelings and insight. Be careful to let your subordinate leader know this is your intent, that it is passive gathering of information and not an inspection or audit. They will be wary of your interaction with their direct reports and worried about their authority being usurped. Play it straight, be consistent, and your subordinate leaders will relax over time. Never use this technique to launch investigations or unilaterally override a subordinate leader's policies or decisions. This turns you into a detective and if that happens everyone will clam up and protect themselves.

Crowdsourcing Insight Externally

Crowdsourcing can be active or passively pursued by a leader. In the passive approach, a leader can seek answers from anywhere he or she chooses. There are often too many sources of information so this passive approach can be time consuming. Examples of active crowdsourcing are crowdsourcing funds to support specific causes, crowdsourcing reviews on Yelp, or crowdsourcing design concepts.

The active approach can be more efficient than passively seeking thought pieces associated with your industry or business, but I still do it coupled with leveraging specific platforms that focus specifically on what I need to learn or understand. As with all such channels of information or support, you should use them to enable you, not drive your behaviors. Remember, you are a leader, so lead.

Do What Works

I advocate using both internal and external, active, and passive resources derived from crowdsourcing to augment your internal reports and formal data analysis. Leveraging the crowdsourced input is a matter of keeping an open mind to a different way to succeed. Absorbing more input only to stay the course based on tradition and a fear of trying something new, defeats the purpose.

Yes, you might find that asymmetrical, informally accessed opinions reinforce your views and those of your team, but that isn't the objective. Resist the temptation to game this effort by targeting internal or external sources that you know agree with the status quo or your policies. Take the risk of finding out that you might be wrong. Practice this exercise with professional humility and you will be the better for doing so.

My direct reports often don't realize the amount of time I spend on nights, in the morning before the sun rises, and on weekends, engaged in data collection, opinion seeking, and yes, openminded thought. Dictate if you must, rarely apply compromise, and practice consensus to refine recommendations coming your way, then decide.

Chapter Sixteen

Blank Slate Leadership

"Attitude is a choice. Happiness is a choice. Optimism is a choice. Kindness is a choice. Giving is a choice. Respect is a choice. Whatever choice you make makes you. Choose wisely."
Roy T. Bennett

Do you see someone new in your organization as a threat, a valuable resource, a competitor? I've observed all three reactions in my peers, subordinates and even superiors in my lifetime. When I was young I could be influenced by the way others thought, all Naval Academy graduate SEAL officers were snobs, all SEALs from the south were great shots, all guys from California were laid back, you get the picture.

Learning to take each person as they presented themselves, to experience regular interaction and eventually, yes to judge them on their merits or lack thereof, was a maturation process that took several years. I had to overcome the pressure to conform to the opinion of others and to evolve a personal and professional belief system that was strong enough to survive nonconformity and social pressure.

When I went to live with my dad in Honolulu, Hawaii, I found myself going from an all-white high school in Nebraska to a high school with less than one hundred white students. The wide range of Asian-Americans, Filipino, Japanese, Taiwanese, and others, made up most of the student population. An additional forty percent were Hawaiian, Samoan, and Tongan. My parents never uttered a racist comment growing up and my friends in Nebraska were uniformly the same, so I wasn't prepared for what happened.

I was a fast kid. My dad held many track records in high

school and in college and that genetic trait passed down to me. Upon arrival at my new school in Hawaii, I tried to join the varsity football team. I'd played football every year since I was ten years old. I loved the game. But the head coach, a native Hawaiian, didn't want me on the team. My dad intervened with the school principal and I was forced onto the team, I'd made an enemy of the head coach, who I found out later, wasn't fond of having white kids on his team.

Hawaii was a strange place. The school was made up of so many ethnic groups it was confusing to a kid from Nebraska. Each group stayed in a close knit social structure barring any relationships across the groups. I spoke to an Asian American girl after class in the hallway one time and an hour later was surrounded by five guys warning me not to talk to their people. In retrospect, I could have become resentful and even bore prejudices for the rest of my life, but that didn't happen.

At the first football practice I attended the coaches quickly realized I was the fastest guy on the field. The defensive coach, a huge Japanese American who'd played college ball, earmarked me for the defensive cornerback position and until the day of the first game I prepared to play that position. The game jerseys were issued at noon on the day of the first game. I waited in line with the other players but when I stepped up to the window the student issuing game jerseys shook his head. There was a note from the head coach. Strong doesn't get a game jersey.

I was dumbfounded but then I realized it was payback for my dad using the principal to get me on the team. I turned around to leave, but a hand shot out and grabbed me. A native Hawaiian with shoulder length hair and wide shoulders stood there, smiling. He was our team's star running back and I knew he was too injured to play out first game of the season. He told he was going to get me a game jersey. I felt the wave of anger and then sadness wash over me as he walked away. Hawaii sucked.

I slogged through the rest of the school day then after class went to the pre-game warm up. I was resigned to wearing street clothes and sitting on the bench. Would I even be allowed to do that? I was sitting in a corner of the locker room, miserable and feeling sorry for myself when the star running back found me and tossed onto my lap, it was a varsity jersey!

I looked up to see he wasn't wearing his game jersey. He smiled at me and said I was a part of the team, that I deserved a jersey, and that I deserved to play. He revealed he'd spoken to the defensive coach and together they decided I'd wear his number, number twenty-four, for the first game of the season.

When I trotted out the head coach saw me and became furious. In just a few days I'd experienced one example of prejudice countered by an act of selfless kindness. Many people suffer greatly from prejudice and my small dose didn't set me back or ruin my life, but it did change my life at a critical moment when I could have easily decided people who didn't look like me or thought like me, were the enemy.

It was after this experience at the age of sixteen, that I decided to judge people based on their behavior and not based on a stereotype or peer pressure. From that day on I strived to see everyone as a blank slate beginning with a perfect score, a glass entirely full. I would evaluate relationships, both personal and professional, by waiting and watching to see if they chipped away at that assessment or held it true by the way they behaved and performed.

Blank slate leadership is applying this principle to people in general as a way of leading and assessing human performance, but it is also a way to approach challenges and solution design. Fresh ideas are often crushed by prejudicial hierarchies in companies, not necessarily because of ethnicity, but because of youth and a traditional requirement that with tenure comes the privilege to speak and to influence.

Baggage

I'm susceptible to prejudice, opinion, attitude, and a whole host of behavioral drivers that could, if I allowed them to, modify my present and future leadership actions. My experiences in Hawaii and in the military proved to me that my epiphany at age sixteen was valid, people are what they are, not what labels others place on them. I learned another hard lesson during my early days in the SEAL Teams. Youth wasn't a virtue. In the military, as in many professions, tenure was king. Military rank is based on tenure defined by years of service. There were a few that jumped the line, but it was rare.

When I joined SEAL Team Two I became a student of the older, more experienced SEALs and listened to their stories over and over to glean the lessons learned, techniques and tactics, that had made them so effective in Vietnam. These were rule breakers, the original disrupters. Whatever worked was worth trying, at least in Vietnam. By the time I joined the SEALs in the late 1970s, these veterans were in their early thirties. They were now senior enlisted men, tenured experts, repeating everything they'd learned before 1972.

I trod lightly, or at least I thought I did at the time, but soon I gained a reputation for questioning the status quo. I did so respectfully but too frequently for these hardened war heroes. There was no way I could gain credibility, the war was over, but there were things that could have been improved, refined. A sea change occurred around 1980 in the SEALs. Many of the original SEALs began retiring, opening slots for more and more new blood.

Around the same time the missions began to change too, Artic warfare, enemy ship attacks, and over the horizon infiltration by air dropped rubber boat. We still had jungle warfare responsibilities, but the new mission areas were wide open to experimentation. I began to have influence along with many of the other young, non-Vietnam veteran SEALs.

For three years raising your hand to ask a question, or God forbid, injecting an idea, was not only frowned upon but grounds for grave concern about your reliability. I learned what it was like to be considered stupid based on age and "inexperience" and I vowed to discontinue the tradition of suppressing new ideas and new people, if I ever became a SEAL leader.

Even today, these memories come rushing to the forefront when I witness senior leaders ignoring young insight and ideas. I can't be everywhere, but I can foster a work culture that is mature enough to allow for wild thoughts and inspirations to enter into the conversations. You don't have to agree or even act, but you should be willing to listen and pay attention. If you have been a victim of this form of discrimination you understand what I'm saying. If you are a traditionalist holding onto the past because you are an expert *in the past*, you need to drop that baggage and wake up. You cannot be a nimble leader and seek creative solutions looking in the rear-view mirror all the time.

Objectivity

Objectivity is difficult to pull off for all the reasons discussed and a whole slew of other behavioral drivers. Habits are behavioral patterns, and they are a source of comfort and security for most of us. Risk taking, in any form, challenges our patterns of behavior. Casting aside those comfortable habits is the first thing an objective leader must do when faced with the unknown. Clear out the rubbish and the history lessons and listen openly, sincerely, and objectively to new input.

Processes and systems are not based on the objective reasoning required today and tomorrow; they are based on the objective reasoning of the past. Show me a process, an organizational chart, or a supporting system and I'll be able to find out pretty quickly what year they were established and in what market or operational environment they were implemented. I think you see the issue here. An over reliance on these management structures become habits and eventually habits become tradition.

I shake things up quite a bit. My folks would tell you I shake things up too much. Maybe that's true, but I do this because I look at decisions as objectively as possible. Champions of this process, or that system, are just that, advocates for the status quo. Strive to create a management communications methodology that embraces crazy new, while respecting the applicable logic of established conventions. Facilitate objectivity by breaking down the advocacy groups and gaining their trust. Objectivity is the first step to validity (and operational sanity).

I've found many leaders understand this philosophy in theory but lose sight of its value once in the trenches. They abhor change and celebrate stability. So do their direct reports, and often all for the sake of stability. This is a dangerous path. As discussed in the chapter about Black Swans, ignoring young, fresh ideas and concepts, being a bull headed advocate for the status quo, and refusing to step back, drop the baggage and think objectively, is the reason Black Swans are a surprise to so many businesses. Be nimble, be objective.

Judgement and Fairness

When bright young people are ignored and their ideas are tossed aside as foolishness, it feels unfair to them. Sure, most entry level professionals have book learning and maybe a smattering of industry related experience, but you know that already. Why be threatened by this desire to help? This is true for any employee or subordinate leader who has an off the wall insight. You'll be amazed at how many enlightened, objective thinkers you have in your company if you just give them half a chance.

We see it in the younger employees but this pent-up motivation to fix and improve things is not an age-related passion. The problem is tradition. The longer a person lives under a regime the more they cope, compensate, and comply. It's time for you to create a culture where people feel comfortable tossing out thoughts, large and small, for consideration. Of course, not every idea is a winner, but I guarantee you it's better to have hundreds of ideas and half-baked solutions to choose from than to look at a conference room filled with silent, compliant prisoners of the past.

Kickstarting this type of engagement is tricky. Your leaders must be involved, and they must want the new culture to succeed. You must establish the ground rules and make it clear that intolerance is the enemy of innovation. You must show them how to be fair minded when hearing new ideas, regardless of the source, regardless of the logic of the thoughts. No great idea springs from the head of a person fully formed into a battle plan. Ideas often flash by in bits, and pieces, and parts, unorganized but many times tantalizingly attractive.

Another aspect of blank slate leadership is judgment. Did my high school coach display sound judgement when he punished me for joining the team? Did the Vietnam veterans show good judgement when they told the new SEALs to stop thinking, shut up, and learn? Hold yourself and your subordinate leaders accountable for good judgement. Sound judgement and fairness can go a long way to ensuring objectivity and creativity thrive. Try it!

Wisdom

Every martial arts movie that comes out of Asia has a wise, white haired master who is the repository of all the collective wisdom and knowledge of his art, in most cases, kung fu. This character is a staple in these movies, and he represents a fact of life, there are those who have lived, loved, lost, and won, and more importantly, survived to become special. Wisdom is precious because it is costly. Most never gain wisdom without great sacrifice and many perish before attaining this lofty attribute.

If you believe that wisdom is the sum total of all your mistakes your aligned with my interpretation. Wisdom is collective pain, and a wise person is the reservoir storing that pain. The phrase "no pain no gain" is appropriate here. Wisdom therefore takes time. It's not necessarily a matter of age though, a seven-year-old tossed on the street, parentless and unsupported, could gain great wisdom by the time they were twenty-one years old. An employee or leader who survived multiple repetitions of a stressful project process might gain five years' worth of wisdom in a condensed time frame. Age is not the way to identify wisdom.

Wisdom expresses itself in subtle ways. Objectivity born of multiple attempts at irrational exuberance, or maybe poise derived from experiencing countless obstacles and challenges. Wisdom is valuable because it implies grounded intelligence. Not book learning, not Ivy League pedigrees, but functional intelligence, sharpened on the rough stone of failure. Being averse to objectivity reduces the opportunities to grow wise through risk taking.

Suppressing oblique insights from people you don't respect due to age, or tenure, or educational background, results in leaders treading water, masters of what they know and little else. To become wise, you must take calculated risks, you must have the courage to fail, and you must learn from your failures and push on. It's scary, I know, I take calculated risks everyday as a CEO, and not all of my calls pan out. I am wise enough to know staying in the fight and taking risks is making me stronger, wiser and in the end more valuable to my company and my board.

Fast Forward Life

I don't hold grudges. I've had adversaries and I'll confess it didn't feel good to have someone misrepresent my performance or my intentions, but I roll with it and toss the negative feelings aside. My experience in Hawaii turned out to be a great time in my life. My best friend was a Jamaican American (there were even fewer African Americans in my school than white kids) and we became close. I learned how to surf and relax a little. But the most important life lesson I took away from Hawaii was my new rule, everyone was good to go until they proved, through bad behavior, that they weren't.

Can you imagine a life where viewing all people as evil, or bad, or prejudiced, was the first instinct? I can't. Sure, I run into these tightly wound people occasionally, they're out there, but I stay far away from their negativity. These people live a cynical and fearful existence, always waiting for someone to do them wrong. A sad existence and outlook, for sure. This life philosophy is certainly not a recipe for creative thinking let alone, creative leadership.

Of course, I've been cheated, lied to, divorced, robbed, beat up, even shot at (not in America), yet I do not paint *all people* the same tint of gray based on these negative memories. You can make the same decision; the choice is yours. Choose to view people in a positive light or as a negative element. In my opinion, the troublesome employee, the struggling junior leader with the attitude, a grumpy shortsighted boss, they all deserve a blank slate. Be the better soul and take the ethical high ground. Drop any negative preconceived notions and take a deep breath. A life filled with positive possibilities is a great life.

I live a *fast forward life*. A life focused on challenges now and in the future. Past is not prologue, especially in business and I believe enlightened leaders can shape their own destiny if they choose to break free from tradition and status quo thinking. Lean forward, faster! Think in loops by zooming in, then zooming out, to gauge the landscape and see the opportunities shimmering on the horizon. Who cares where you went to school, who cares if you were a SEAL, the best athlete, or the project lead on a great success story, *it's old news!*

Humility breeds a hunger to be ready, to be smarter, to know what is true, now, not last year or five years ago. Humility keeps the nimble leader on his or her toes. A healthy thought is that there's a competitor out there somewhere working harder, working smarter than you are. I wake up ready to engage the future. I take what lessons the past can provide, especially regarding human nature, but I do not use the path to where I am to take me to where I need to be tomorrow.

You can embrace the *fast forward life* philosophy too! Take a deep breath and decide you will give credence to history to apply twenty percent of yesterday's context and eighty percent focusing on the new game and the nature of the fight at hand, when making decisions. Innovation is born from this mindset. Creativity too. If you want to excel as a leader become objective, wise, and humble and lean into the storm! It's more rewarding than dangerous, take my word for it!

Chapter Seventeen

Leading Through Adversity

> *"Start by doing what's necessary; then do what's possible; and suddenly you are doing the impossible."*
> **Francis of Assisi**

The heavy weight boxer, Mike Tyson famously said, "Everybody's got a plan until they get punched in the face." I agree. To demonstrate Mike Tyson was onto something, I give you the German Field Marshal known as Moltke the Elder, who said in the late 1800s, "No plan of operations extends with certainty beyond first contact with the enemy." Seeing a trend here?

Adversity is defined as either difficulty or misfortune. The first is a staple of life and business. The second is plain and simple, bad luck. Whether your adversity is derived from hard times or karma, you need to understand it is a part of the deal if you want to be a successful leader. Nimble leadership gives you a fighting chance. Nimble leaders are open to change, agile enough to take a punch or side slip one. They are creative and proactive, so they make their own luck by applying sweat, tears, and intellect, to change the course of their destiny. The ancient Roman philosopher, Lucius Seneca, said, "Luck is when preparation meets opportunity." I think the ancient Romans were on to something.

In my chapter dedicated to Black Swan events, I pointed out that being ready for change is half the battle to avoiding most Black Swans. Seneca was right, mental, physical, and organizational preparation will help inoculate you to the misfortune brought on by ignorance, apathy, and arrogance. What about dealing with old fashioned hardship? Is there a cure for that ailment?

Hardship is like the wind or the rain, elemental constants in life and a part of performing any challenging task. Consider a concert violinist. Long years dedicated to practicing the craft before arriving at the top of the game. Or a prima ballerina, toes mangled and bleeding all the way to the top of the marque. You see my point. Struggle, pain, setbacks, and hardship are the price of winning and excelling.

What scars do leaders have? Can we see them as they walk by or stand in front of us each day? Well, they're there for sure, but most of the leadership scar tissue is on the inside, unseen and often, unappreciated. Mental anguish, tension, fear, apprehension, sleepless nights, and other silent enemies work to tear down the energy, commitment, and motivation of leaders. These forms of friction and resistance compete to bring leaders down, or at least numb them into apathy.

On the Ropes

All leaders, the bad, the good, and the great, suffer through failure. Failure isn't fun and that's the point. To fail you must strive to achieve and short of that, to learn. The task must be worthwhile or there is no value in the experience, win, lose, or draw. Still this method of learning is a bitter pill to swallow.

A rough stone may produce a sharper blade, but the blade must endure the trial to achieve the desired outcome. You need to come to grips with this concept. As a leader you will be tested, you will be punished, and you will fail. It's what you do with that failure that makes all the difference.

Navy SEAL training pops up on television from time to time showing shivering young men lifting logs or lugging black rubber boats, while athletic looking instructors scream at them. At most, the images last twenty to thirty seconds. As a former graduate of that endurance course, and former SEAL instructor, I shake my head when I see these quick descriptions of what some call the toughest military training in the world. Twenty to thirty seconds doesn't do it justice.

Here's the truth. SEAL students do lift logs and boats, but they do it for hours and hours, and during Hell Week they do it for days. That's right, days. Why does this elite course focus so much on the delivery of pain? It's actually simple and straightforward. In war, a SEAL unit will suffer far greater physical and mental trauma than legally allowable in SEAL training. All SEALs know that. The students are only required to prove they can endure fifty percent of what's to come, should they be sent overseas to fight. Their pain is only the beginning of their learning curve in dealing with adversity.

In World War II most elite forces didn't survive long. Great rewards require great risks and usually result in dramatic losses in wartime. SEAL training and other U.S. elite military training courses create a simulated combat environment full of stress to test the mettle of each student. It must work, SEALs have accomplished incredible feats of valor and audacity as a direct result of this elite screening process since 1962.

The SEAL course is the metaphorical rough stone and the number of successful students it produces each year is meager at best. Of thousands who apply, only a few hundred are chosen to begin the grueling experience, and only a handful of those graduate and become Navy SEALs. The crucible of Leadership is similar in that the risks you take, the failure and pain you experience, the embarrassment and setbacks you endure are both preparation for, and a test of, *your mettle.*

I can't say SEAL training was more difficult that other struggles in my life, they were different tests, but they oddly delivered the same level of debilitating pain. Losing friends in training and in combat, losing a young son, having cancer twice, and yes, failing repeatedly as a leader over the years on my way to wisdom.

Each setback, each traumatic event, hit me hard and created pain that, in many cases, lingered on for years. I've become stronger through it all and while the journey was arduous, I've come back off the ropes swinging so often I now understand that pain and suffering are an unavoidable prerequisite to gaining wisdom, patience, and empathy. As the nineteenth century German philosopher, Friedrich Nietzsche, observed, "What does not kill me makes me stronger." He nailed it!

Scaling Down to Survive

There has been a lot written about the challenges of scaling young companies faced with great opportunities and insatiable demand for their products and services. I enjoy this type of upward scaling; it's associated with winning and the exhilaration that comes with rising success. The other kind of scaling, downward, isn't nearly as fun or rewarding but it is a consequence of adversity, both in business and in life.

In the earlier chapters I focused on building, not dismantling a company structure. I covered organizational design, position design, development or reassessment of key processes and systems. I discussed hiring or transitioning the right people into the new structure, and finally, I indicated how training, coaching, and mentoring can lock in the new normal and set a tone and basis for success across the entire company. If you plan to successfully scale down you must follow these same guidelines and yes, you must unravel much of what took you so long to create in order to survive long enough to grow again.

As I write this, the COVID-19 pandemic has ravaged many businesses in the United States. Mandated shutdowns, travel restrictions, and limited desire by employees and patrons to engage freely in work and commerce have resulted in the shuttering of tens of thousands of companies, never to return. However, the adversity that drives downward scaling doesn't have to be biblical in proportions to be emotionally and physically draining for a leader. How do you cope?

First, as discussed in the chapter on Black Swan events, it

is how quickly you accept and decide to adapt to the negative change that gives you a fighting chance. Second, realize it will be tough on you, regardless of your game face, leaders feel personally responsible for their companies and any event or series of events that threaten their cherished ward creates fear, denial, anger, and in some cases, a severe loss of self-confidence.

Of course, everyone in the business will be feeling many of these same emotions but good leaders know they are the accountable person. The buck stops with them and this understanding can either demoralize or energize leaders faced with adversity. If you've lived through this, you know what I'm saying is true. It's lonely to contemplate your failures, even if the failure was only based on bad timing, such as taking the reins of leadership just before a worldwide pandemic. Regardless of the reasons, it's time to be the leader the moment demands.

Lead, Follow, or Get Out of the Way

Adversity is a part of the world we live in. When doing your periodic leader capabilities self-survey, ask yourself if you are ready for disasters, large and small to strike. I believe that about half of all leaders fail to anticipate the downside and waltz along naively until the day comes, and it will come, when the world tilts and the business starts to fall apart.

Here are a few of the odd crisis leadership behaviors I've observed: denial of the problem, shooting the messenger, blaming anyone, blaming everyone, and shutting down. You've seen these behaviors too I imagine, and surprisingly, it doesn't take a major life and death disaster to stimulate these poor leadership reactions.

If you can mentally prepare for the bad news moment, train for it through mental visualization, or even gaming out negative scenarios with others, you will likely avoid exhibiting these bad behaviors. Will preparation turn you into a fearless pillar of strength when the time comes? Maybe not, but it will help you to be in the top twenty five percent of leaders who do not melt down, or torch everyone and everything in sight. Poor leaders invariably do whatever it takes to distance themselves from accountability for the mess. Don't allow adversity to defeat you.

Preparation is essential but so is time in the fire. The more often you either observe good or poor leaders in crisis, or perform as a leader in crisis, the more scar tissue and experience you gain and that, plus preparation, gets you into the top quartile of leaders. The way to lead through adversity is to bring a mix of your skills and strengths and the strength of the organization you've built, to survive.

How healthy is your company? Is it robust and resilient? Are your subordinate leaders also preparing and gaming scenarios in preparation? Do you have resource contingences well in hand? You've heard this in earlier chapters, but it is the essence of great leadership to have a well-trained and philosophically aligned team at your back when the crap hits the fan.

There are times when you should allow another leader or technical expert to call the shots. Imagine a ticking bomb sitting on the floor of your office. Do you attempt to diffuse the device, or do you call in a bomb disposal expert? Following or deferring to their expert guidance in this case is smart leadership on your part.

Grinder Time

As of this writing it is popular in business to admire those who grind. The term reflects the positive attributes of self-sacrifice, hard work, and thoroughness. A blue collar work ethic. If you are a grinder you are a hero in the company. Interestingly, in the SEALs the term also refers to a place of physical torture, the rectangular slab of rough concrete that occupies the center of the SEAL basic training compound in Coronado, California.

The grinder is where we trained, where we were punished, individually, as boat crews, or as a class for our weaknesses.

That sacred location holds a special place in the hearts of all SEAL graduates and those who aspired to become SEALs because we all shared the experience and value the results of that experience.

The punishment and torture go away after the first nine weeks of SEAL training but admiration for those who work hard and succeed through a dedication to hard work is valued for the rest of their lives. Adversity can be a short duration grind, or it can be an exercise in endurance. Grinding all the time or for long periods of time isn't healthy. It may be a symptom, a reflection of understaffing or systemic failures that can't be overcome with only blood, sweat, and tears. Grinding also means, to wear down.

Remember the adage, work smarter not harder? Make sure your grinders are working smart, too. Don't take them for granted, either. Especially in challenging times. They may not be able to sustain this laudable work ethic indefinitely. Don't let those around them lean on them too much, either. That goes for you too. Relying on the heroic effort of a few can contribute to creating weaknesses in your team and ultimately, failure.

My SEAL training class started with one hundred and twenty-six, handpicked, heavily screened and motivated, young men. Within five weeks the class was down to thirty-six students and a clear *grinder* had emerged. In the physical sense my classmate Joe was a beast. He'd been rolled into our class after getting injured in a previous SEAL training class, He was older, he was charismatic, and his energy pulsed through our class during every training event. He helped the weak, cheered up the sad, and was one of the top athletic performers. Joe was a natural leader.

The crucible of BUD/S training is a five-day period known as "Hell Week". The class is separated into rubber boat crews of seven men each. The boat crews are forced to compete against each other, against time, and against the elements. They do this for small favors and prizes, like five minutes of sleep, or being warm. There is almost no sleep during Hell Week and the instructor teams rotate regularly so they are sharp and fresh even as the SEAL class slides deeper and deeper into physical and psychological distress.

I wasn't in Joe's boat crew. I was in the "Smurfs", the traditional name for the boat crew composed of the shortest students. On Wednesday morning of my Hell Week, around two in the morning, we arrived at the base dining facility known as a chow hall. The rubber boats were staged outside in the parking lot and a student was placed on guard. The guard was rotated every fifteen minutes. When the first guard was relieved, he walked into the chow hall and remained silent until he sat down at a table full of tired classmates. He leaned close and whispered, "Joe just quit!"

Within seconds the news swept the room and the shock on everyone's face was apparent. Not Joe! Nothing could hurt Joe! Apparently, as we shuffled toward the chow hall with the rubber boats poised painfully on the tops of our heads, Joe's neck muscles pinched a nerve so painfully he couldn't handle it anymore. As we all lowered the boats and shuffled into the chow hall focused on food and a short rest from walking, none of us saw Joe standing back, talking to an instructor and then to a medical specialist. Joe couldn't or wouldn't go on, so he said the words, I quit, and they took him back across the street.

The affect was unexpected, but it shouldn't have been. As soon as the meal was over and we went outside to get our boats, four students quit. Several others tried but were talked back into the class by the instructors. As far as these students were concerned, if Joe couldn't do this, I can't do this! I remembered this lesson for a long time.

When I was a SEAL training instructor almost a decade later, I saw this phenomenon unfold in SEAL classes repeatedly. The class officers as well as the students happily tapped into the hero's energy and went dormant, willing to be pulled along by someone else's force of will and strength. I broke this party up as often as I could and tried to inspire the leaders to take risks and lead by example, be that enthusiastic voice, to not become over reliant on the few grinders that were carrying the heart of the class in their pocket. You see where I'm going with this.

Joe came back to BUD/S two years later, graduated, and became a great SEAL operator. I don't know if he ever knew the effect, positive at first then negative, he had on my class but what held true then, in that context, holds true today. Leaders and peers who lean heavily on star performers, the grinders, are setting the business up for a shock. When adversity strikes these heroes grind harder and burn out faster, leaving the rest of the team ill prepared for the issues at hand. Build a grinder culture that relies of a team of heroes, not over reliance on a precious few.

Outliving the Competition

Putting together all the tips, tools, tricks, and strategies discussed in this book will help you endure adversity. You will get stronger, wiser, and be better able to guide the rest of your people through the crucible, whatever form it takes. You'll live with, and live through bad bosses, irrational partners, weak subordinates, and your own failures. I've found that nimble and creative leadership forces me to revive my capabilities, shores up my strengths and eliminates my weaknesses. Like a phoenix I rise from the ashes of one crisis, stronger, wiser. I persevere and live to fight another day.

During my military career, my seven years in financial services, my fifteen years in government contracting and my five years and counting in healthcare, I strived to be a change agent. I'm aware I may have made enemies of those too entrenched to see the obvious future, and I watched most of these naysayer's fade into obscurity over time as things *did change*. There is redemption in survival. If you embrace the nimble spirit you will look back at your years of passionate pleading and arguing and realize your instincts were spot on, your gut instinct was correct.

I wasn't always right, of course, but since I leaned forward and challenged the status quo I was positioned to be right more often than wrong, in the future. It sucks in the present when nobody can see what you so plainly see, but it is the nature of people to disbelieve what they don't *already* understand. Be patient. In time you will outperform and outlive your naysayers and if you follow the guidance in this book, you will have inspired and guided a new generation of nimble leaders spreading creativity and disruption everywhere they go in your memory. Endure, evolve, persevere!

Chapter Eighteen

The Only Easy Day Was Yesterday

"There's an inherent danger in letting people think that they have perfected something. When they believe they've 'nailed it,' most people tend to sit back and rest on their laurels while countless others will be laboring furiously to better their work!"
Richard Branson

Painted on the wall over the pullup bars in the BUD/S training compound in Coronado, California, are the words, *The Only Easy Day Was Yesterday*. New students stare up at this riddle every morning while executing thousands of pushups, sit-ups, jumping jacks, and pull-ups. What does the phrase mean? Instructors pick out students and ask the question, but few ever guess the key to understanding humility, at least not at first.

I speak to this topic throughout this book because it is what shapes the story of my personal and professional success. Humility is why elite teams, in and out of the military context, violate the accepted, mundane performance metrics that many people settle for. These low performance measures are often crafted to limit expectations, to reduce the stress of failure, and improve morale through mediocrity. To dare to break the rules is audacity, to forget what you know and seek new knowledge requires humility.

The phrase painted on the wall in Coronado could mean that today's going to be tougher than yesterday, so get ready! On the surface that's what many young SEAL students agree is the meaning of the riddle. However, there is a deeper meaning. The sacred message of the riddle is to start every day with an open mind and cast aside your ego and your accolades. Nobody cares what you achieved in the past, it's time to show up and prove your value all over again.

SEALs are heroic, intelligent, and lauded by the public. They receive hundreds and hundreds of military decorations for courage under fire and succeeding on missions that are truly impossible. Yet, every day SEALs come into work and feel the paranoia of not being good enough, not yet. That's what drives them to learn, to grow, to overcome, paranoia. They can't afford to rest on their laurels because a potential adversary out there somewhere is training harder, getting faster, getting smarter.

Over time raw paranoia transitions to studied self awareness and acceptance of humility as a secret weapon. The naïve attempt to master everything eventually gives way to a calmer understanding of how the game must be played. Like wisdom, humility is a trait gained through experience, sometimes failure, and sometimes success. In my experience, the easy days are always behind me. When that stops being the case, I'll either be bored out of my mind, or dead.

This chapter will delve into the methods you can use to apply humility in ways that, hopefully, will prepare you for leadership in a way that ensures repeatable success. I may use more military references in this chapter than usual, but the applications of these methods are not restricted to the military environment or military tasks and objectives. I've experienced all the effects of humility and lack thereof, in business as well as in uniform.

Battle Rhythm

The military, especially the ground forces of the U.S. Army and the United States Marine Corps, have a concept they teach to leaders called battle rhythm. Oddly, the term is not easily defined and open to some interpretation. It can be understood in the military context as the planned cycle of command and planned staff and unit activities, organized preemptively, to better prepare for the next phase of operations. Earlier in this book I used the example of an infantry squad taking a key hill position. An appropriate application of battle rhythm in that example would express itself once the hill was taken by the squad.

The young officer must establish his new position in anticipation of an enemy counterattack. He places his men in a perimeter, he scans in the direction of the fleeing enemy to ascertain their intent, and to perhaps spot a second enemy force staging for an attack. He then receives headcount, ammunition status and casualty information from his Sergeant who's trained to perform this task as soon as a position is taken, or an enemy assault has ended.

The young officer calls in the status of his squad, any enemy insights he has, requests additional resources as needed, and then settles in, awaiting an attack or new orders. The Sargent ensures the ammunition is redistributed, he directs every other soldier to drink and eat, and then rest, establishing a schedule for these activities, then reports completion of this to the officer. The squad waits. The rotation of guard duty continues. The squad is resupplied, and maybe injured soldiers are recovered by a helicopter. The squad waits. Then new orders arrive, take the next hill!

In war, there can be countless hills, countless objectives. Taking one or three or twenty doesn't get you off the hook. You just keep doing the job until it's over. Humility serves to prepare everyone to expect the unexpected, to set up for the next attack or the next mission assignment. There's no resting on laurels in this scenario. And if you think about it, resting on your laurels after any success isn't prudent in business either.

A leader who prepares for the battle rhythm of their business or workflow environment is a leader who will be ready for the next struggle. Apply the methods used by the young officer to your situation, to your team. After a hard three weeks finishing a big project do you immediately capture lessons learned? Do you immediately bonus the heroes and praise the team? Do you give the team a few days off, maybe a long weekend to replenish their energy mentally and physically? If not, why not?

If you push from one extreme performance output situation to the next, you will burn people out, you will find yourself falling short of critical support resources, and you will begin to fail. You can specifically identify the key people or workhorses that are more likely to get battle fatigue and flame out on you. For example, if you only have one competent proposal team lead and you're happily pitching major proposals right and left, maybe you should double up on that critical position.

If there's a choke point or single point of failure (people or systems and equipment) maybe you should create redundancy so if something does break (or someone) your capability or capacity to produce results doesn't suddenly end. Earlier we reviewed the value of proactively evaluating crisis scenarios to determine these weak points and the logic behind building resiliency and redundancy.

If you've followed this philosophy, you may be okay when a surge in critical work hits the business. Be prepared, and if you find yourself in the middle of a battle and the wheels are starting to fall off, fix the issues in real-time, then make it a rule to be ready for next time. Pace and poise under fire results in endurance and eventual success.

Leaders Need Rest Too

We're going to talk about how to take care of yourself at length in the next chapter, but it bears noting here. Leaders are people too. They are usually the apex point of concentrated authority, and possibly wisdom and knowledge, at least on a broader scale. What happens if you prepare and plan, and stage, and train, and your team executes brilliantly, repeatedly, but all the while you breakdown physically and mentally as a result? If there is only one you in the mix, there are a few things you can do to alleviate this form of concentration risk.

Empowering your subordinate leaders and their technical performers is scary but at the same time liberating. You should always be careful about financial controls, release, and access to money, and the use of money (raises, bonuses, etc.), but limiting these and other classic control areas to one leader is a recipe for disaster. Picture your organization operating without your permission. Can they? Evaluate this and decide if smart policies mandating behaviors and liabilities is a better answer than holding all the keys in your sweaty grip.

Do as much of this as possible. Assign others to be the backups in specific situations. Use your CFO or senior financial person as a check and balance against fraud and abuse of authority. Free up the communications flow so it doesn't all flow through you. Establish horizontal communications, reporting, and execution processes for critical workflows and projects. This simple act will free up your time and your mind and put the onus for successful performance on the people working the challenges.

Another method to consider is the use of an empowered special leader. A leader that is temporarily empowered to execute and lead a specific task or project. The U.S. Government uses "Czars" to tackle difficult, cross-governmental issues that are temporary in nature. Your version of this does not have to have a royal title to be effective. They need your support and the resources to win. They will also need you to run interference for them as they bang up against traditions, change resistance, and jealousy.

As a young Navy Lieutenant, I was asked to write a thought piece, that if impactful, might save the Navy's mini-submarine program. The paper worked and I found myself swept up in controversy. Many of the senior SEAL leaders were against the points I raised and the solution I presented, but the Admiral in charge of all the SEALs in the Navy approved of my approach and gave me a year to put my words into practice and prove I was correct.

I started out knowing the Admiral was supportive and hopeful. I also began with a whole host of new enemies I'd never met. I struggled for the first six months of this endeavor and was sure it would fail as everything I needed was denied me by multiple layers of SEAL leadership positioned between me and the Admiral. I was going to own defeat and through no fault of my own, look like a usurper to many senior leaders in my community. Then I received a phone call and all that changed.

Three months into the effort I was told there was a message for me to call a SEAL Captain in California. I was working on the new project in Virginia and was curious why a senior west coast SEAL wanted to speak with a lowly junior officer. After the call, I was both elated and fearful. The Admiral was aware of the obstruction campaign against me and had ordered the east coast SEAL leaders to stop their games and immediately provide Strong whatever he needed to succeed. Sounds good right?

I was able to accelerate the project with all that clout behind me and eventually the proof of concept created changes in the mini-submarine program and the SEAL teams that are still in place today. My enemies didn't forget though, and instead of seeing their behaviors as the problem, they saw me as the upstart that caused them pain and a loss of face with the Admiral.

I won the battle, but they wouldn't let me win the war. It was a small community at the time, less than two thousand SEALs. I don't regret my role in the success of my idea but I learned a lot about why spirited and consistent sponsorship of a special project leader is critical to not only the project's success, but also their wellbeing in your company after the special project ended. Delegate and then back up your leaders so you have the bandwidth to see the bigger picture and avoid leader burnout!

Financial Security Equals Strength

Another aspect of leader resiliency is personal financial stability.

It is difficult if not impossible to do the right thing if your job is so vital, losing it is tantamount to a personal disaster. You should have the ability to be honest, forthright, brave, and decisive without risking your livelihood but sometimes these leader traits are not seen by senior leaders as a positive and this behavior puts you at risk.

Your disruptive leadership approach, challenging static apathy and rigid human structures, will be seen by many as a threat to what they believe is right or, if they built the house you are renovating, they are upset to watch their work under attack. Being financially stable, having personal savings, solid investments, and low debt will help you maintain your ethical, moral, and professional compass heading throughout the change management cycle.

There is certainly the potential for financial risk in following the tenets of this book simply because nimble leadership is perceived as destructive, before it has a chance to prove it is restorative and enlightening. Being a creative change agent isn't for the faint of heart, trust me.

Since going into the business world, in any scenario where I've been placed in a special leadership position, replaced a traditional leader, or was given near carte blanche to execute, I was still treated by my peers, many senior leaders, and by many subordinates as an illegitimate leader. I've learned over time to trust in my track record and my mission focused approach to making the decisions that I make. I know I'm effective and that the path to optimization is not the path to social acceptance and friendship.

You'll be threatening to most, not because you are mean or terrible, but because you represent change, and they can't see themselves in the future you are describing and building. Personal financial security is a cornerstone that permits you to be the leader you need to be and if it doesn't work out, you can move on knowing you stuck to your guns and did what you knew to be right. Eventually most come around, they just have to see the vision unfold and be successful before understanding and approving of what the madness hath wrought.

Professional S Curve

When you become wildly successful, and I'm sure that you will, you may find that the challenges of yesterday no longer test your capabilities. This is a natural progression for effective leaders and a natural evolutionary process that will require you to take stock of your situation. Should you stay, you may find yourself committing less and less of your ability and energy into leading. Should you seek a new challenge?

If your company has many rungs in the ladder above your current position you only have to evaluate if there's room for you to move up. But if there's little room at the top it may be time to set your sights on a physical change to a new organization that will provide you with room to grow. This isn't easy. When your efforts pay off and the machine you built is humming along, you'll have less stress and less potential for professional failure. It is human nature to chill a little and smell the roses but beware, you're beginning to rest on those darn laurels!

Business schools speak of S curves, the developmental path of a service, product, a company, or even an industry. The trip begins with early innovative ideas then rises as adoption of the idea, product, or service gains notice. Eventually a successful path goes vertical in value as wider excitement creates extraordinary demand. This success pattern, flat for a while before curving up slightly and then radically, is the fabled S curve.

Eventually, the vertical rise is dampened by market resistance, a lack of new buyers, or a new trend. It flattens out and may even decline. The path from innovation to resistance may take years or months depending on the product or service. One way to avoid value resistance is referred to as jumping the

S curve or reinventing the S curve. Simply put, you start a new product or service, and overlap the S curve evolution of your current offering with that of the new thing. You can do this professionally as well.

People can track their professional lives in the same manner. You start as a leader making waves but not a difference. Then your squawking and petitioning gains momentum and your ideas take hold. Suddenly you are advancing, and promotion comes faster and faster until it doesn't. You stagnate and deal with the factors that are blocking further advancement or professional growth. You've hit the resistance and are flatlining. What to do?

Be cognizant of this professional growth path. Observe it and anticipate the resistance. Be ready to move on, either internally or externally by the time the vertical of your professional curve begins to tip over to flat line. While you are doing this reevaluate your strengths and weaknesses then apply them not to your current role, but to the stretch role waiting for you. Don't rest on your success and do not decide you have arrived at the zenith of all knowledge, wisdom, and ability. Be humble, push into the unknown, and grow professionally!

Small, Medium, Large, or Startup?

Where are nimble leaders treated best? In my opinion, the size of the enterprise doesn't matter when it comes to nimble and creative leadership philosophy. What business wouldn't benefit from creative thinking? Startups and small companies can represent great personal financial risk, have limited internal opportunities for upward mobility, but they allow you the opportunity to get in on the ground floor, and make highly impactful decisions. You're a big fish in a small pond.

Medium to large businesses possess more resources, more technical expertise, better underlying support platforms, and more mature systems, processes, and policies. They pay more and have more room for advancement. Maybe you should focus on these opportunities as your next evolutionary step. If financial surety is important to you above all other considerations. You will have to be the judge. Small companies are exhilarating and scary. Large enterprises are safer yet steeped in traditions and adverse to change for any reason.

Establish your own brand of nimble and creative leadership and shape a position description that aligns with your strengths and offers you a path to continued professional learning. Then match that position description to the scenarios presented by small, medium, large, and start-up organizations. This is a good exercise because it helps you to define your brand as a leader and also identifies what situations allow you to have the greatest impact, influence, and satisfaction. Build your next professional S curve and then make it happen!

The Next Act

It might seem strange for me to coach you into leaving the very company I advised you to build throughout this book. I present this to you as a strategy for personal and professional happiness. Do what you can for as long as you can, and if successful, evolve. If you are not successful, evaluate why and evolve. Evolution is about adaptation to new influences, new challenges, and new conditions. Don't rest, don't sit back and stare dreamily at your plaque covered wall. Hide the trophies and get real, you could and should, push to become better, always.

So, what is your next act? Are you spending any time thinking about what the next you will look like? Reinvention is fun if you think of it as long-term strategy. You can grow by doing something entirely different the next time or by incrementally stretching beyond your current position and set of challenges. In either case, you need to be thinking about you and your future. If you do, I believe you'll realize the future is always bright!

Chapter Nineteen

Be Well

"All men dream, but not equally. Those who dream by night in the dusty recesses of their minds, wake in the day to find that it was vanity, but the dreamers of the day are dangerous men, for they may act on their dreams with open eyes, to make them possible."
T.E. Lawrence

This is an aspirational chapter, for me. That's right, I am going to discuss an aspect of nimble leadership that I have not entirely mastered, leader wellness. As a result of walking the walk and learning the craft of leadership, I find myself rarely able to say no to a new challenge. As you gain momentum and wisdom, you gain insights and a calm state of mind that people can see and feel. They know instinctively that you can help them or take on much more of a load than you already have. In my various careers my answer to a request for help was always, yes.

Saying yes to every request, to every task, becomes a habit. A habit that has consequences. Family life suffers, physical health suffers, and mental health and wellness can suffer the most. This chapter reflects on what leaders like you, can do to avoid the pitfalls of stress, embrace techniques and disciplines, and improve your ability and capacity to live a well life, and *still* be a great leader.

You don't have to do everything I suggest, there's more than enough ideas here to counterbalance the oftentimes debilitating drive to succeed professionally. I only ask that you keep an open mind and consider your wellness for a few minutes. This chapter is not about aesthetics. Looking good in the gym or in a suit has value but not necessarily wellness value. I'm talking about getting off the clock, replenishing your vigor, and clearing your mind. Ready?

Stress Release the Old School Way

My dad was average in many ways, and in others not so much. He was a self-taught oil painter, a self-taught musician in five instruments, and could speak passable Vietnamese and Mandarin Chinese. Not bad for an Iowa farm kid who survived the great depression of the 1930s. My dad was, from outward appearances, a successful, middle-class, white-collar worker but the stress of that work drove him to seek relief in a bottle of bourbon on most nights.

He wasn't alone. In the late Twentieth Century, alcohol and drugs were a way to relieve the pressure of life and work. It was also accepted as the way to do just that, relax. My dad was a high school and collegiate athlete who never worked out again after graduating with a degree in accounting. Exercising was for athletes and kids. Real adults suffered in silence and pretended to be well-adjusted by getting trashed on the weekends and tipping a few every night in between.

Oddly enough, my dad was also a student of the Orient. He'd spent time in Vietnam and in Japan and was fascinated by their cultures and their history. He read books about Asian religions, meditation, and even learned to cook Asian cuisine, but he never adopted any of the Asian systems for mental and physical relaxation and wellbeing. I often wonder what his life would have been like if he'd learned Tai Chi, or studied the strategy game, Go. Maybe took up yoga? My dad died too young, a victim of his choices. An intelligent and emotional man who never knew how to take it on the chin and let it go. He was old school until the end.

Now, my kids would say I'm old school too, maybe so, but not in the way my dad was. Perhaps I dodged the bullet because I saw the damage substance abuse, even if its only alcohol, can do to people, even strong people. I did drink heavily for the first few years in the Navy, but it was to be accepted by the older SEALs. They all drank, a lot, and didn't trust anyone who didn't imbibe with them. It was fun, not stress relief.

Most SEAL veterans had post-traumatic stress-disorder from multiple combat tours in Vietnam, even though PTSD wasn't yet a diagnosed illness in the 1970s. Others were just bored with life. They missed the high-octane thrill of living and possibly dying in combat. Normal life was depressing, so they too drank to excess. Old school all the way. I had two habits that I've retained to this day. Habits that helped me to unwind. Reading and working out.

Reading for Enjoyment

My mom was a big reader, so was my dad. It was their passion for reading that gave me a leg up early in school. I don't remember how I got turned on to novels, but I did know by the time I was ten years old. I never went anywhere without a good book tucked away. I read anywhere and everywhere. My early focus was on war. Not modern war, but knights and warriors from an age before gunpowder, an age when arrows were considered a coward's weapon. Then came science fiction, followed by books about mountain men and American Indians.

Once I joined the Navy, I stopped reading novels and started getting serious. I was comfortable learning from books, so I became a consumer of knowledge. About my work as a SEAL, and anything else I thought would make me smart. It was purely vocational and definitely not a stress relief strategy. It wouldn't be until I turned thirty that I rediscovered my old hiding place, I started reading novels again.

The author who pulled me back was Barry Sadler, the man who wrote and recorded the *Ballad of the Green Beret,* in 1966. That song hit number one in the charts and sold over a million records. Sadler was a wounded Green Beret and while that song gained him notoriety it was his writing that drew me to him. He wrote the Casca series of historical adventure novels. Twenty-two books on the life of a Roman soldier doomed to live forever as a soldier by Christ as he died on the cross. I initially read a ragged copy a fellow SEAL handed me, and I was hooked.

Maybe reading isn't for you. Now audio books take the stories and pump them straight into your brain. Movies, streaming content online, any visual and audible transference of *value* that distracts your churning leader mind and gives you respite from constant problem solving, is worth a try. And in this context, *value* equals distraction from the grind. I still find myself mindlessly enjoying shows about UFOs, bigfoot, and lake monsters. I've added treasure hunting to that list. I forget the cares and stresses of the moment and just enjoy. It's very new school.

Escaping the World of Steel and Plastic

A park, a beach, a local field, a stand of trees, the mountains, if it doesn't look and feel like your workplace, go there! We cycle back and forth between steel and plastic environments, manmade and sterile. We don't even look outside at the beauty of nature as we drive to and from our work and home, and back again. We all need a break from sterile, especially busy leaders. Leaders need an infusion of nature from time to time to rest and reestablish a balance.

I'm not insisting you fly to an exotic location, the stress of planning, traveling, and the cost of a major trip, may be counterproductive for our purposes here. Keep it simple but frequent. The Japanese have long understood the peaceful and contemplative healing effect of nature. It doesn't have to be much. A small garden will suffice. If you live in the city and can't create a garden spot go to a public park and find a quiet corner. Soak it in and relax.

Experiential Racing

A few years ago, I went beyond passive interaction with nature, I began competing in experiential events held outdoors. Trail runs, hikes, distance running, obstacle course races, long distance kayaking, fun stuff! In the SEALs the environment isn't your friend. You're always too cold, too wet, too hot, and the distances are always too long. Throw unique terrain into the mix such as swamps, deserts, mountains, and jungles and it all turns into a big bite of pain and misery.

The great outdoors for SEALs *is the office.* I spent many years after retirement staying as far away from bugs, heat, and hunger, as I possibly could. It was a natural reaction to twenty years of getting beat up in the wild, but I eventually realized I was missing the positive elements of being outdoors. So, on a whim and several years after retiring from the Navy, I agreed to enter an adventure race.

Now, these crazy races are more survival events than speed trials. They come in all sizes and shapes, eight hours, twelve hours, twenty-four hours, and longer. Some focus on mountains while others focus on rugged flat terrain. The rules are simple, stay hydrated, take your time studying your map, and do the distance while hunting for specific geographic targets or points. Get lost? That's on you, fix it. Get too beat down to continue? Easy, go to a road and sit down, the race safety patrol will be along shortly to take you back to the starting point.

Outdoor activities of this difficulty may be beyond your resources in time and your level of commitment, but they do keep you humble, trust me. I began these activities in my late forties and continued for several years. They were brutal but exciting and delivered the escape I needed from time to time. I eventually shifted to mountain biking and shorter race events, but I miss those brutal but cleansing twelve-hour challenges.

The key here is the experience. I wasn't able to compete head to head with the Xterra athletes that led each race, nor was I even in the middle of the pack when a race was over. But the experience and the fact it was out of the office or home environment was just what I needed to unwind. Mother Nature doesn't care if you are an ex-SEAL, a CEO, or a graduate from a prestigious university. It's a leveler, all humans must become creative and courageous, when faced with the reality of nature, or suffer the consequences.

Physical Training

I was always a terrible long-distance runner. Give me a track, forty or one hundred meters long, and my family DNA kicked in as I torched the sprint distance. Go any farther and well, I sucked. The worst runner in SEAL training must still pass rigid time and distance tests every week or risk dismissal from the course. I passed the entry requirements for running by two seconds.

I passed all but two of all the timed running events in the course by a similar narrow margin. I was punished weekly for this shortfall by the instructors. I hated running but at the age of fifty I started doing it as a release and an escape from stress. I've never experienced the "runner's high" so I can't attest to how that feels. Running was a job requirement as a SEAL, no more, no less.

When I began running for fun it helped me to focus on other aspects of my heath such as diet, and smart hydration. I've learned that exercising regularly stimulates endorphins and in turn, endorphins give me a light euphoric feeling during and right after my workouts. I've learned how to moderate my workouts, so they are helpful and not destructive. Agility, mobility, some strength training, and a little endurance, these are my basic objectives. Oh yes, and to detox from my stressful career.

Your workouts can take many forms. I've joined bicycle spin clubs, participated in organized training programs in specialized gyms, and I've trained in Muay Thai, the ancient art of Thai boxing. These all took me outside of my normal environment and my comfort zone to both humble me and provide me with a physical and mental edge. You can exercise for as little as twenty minutes a day or longer if you have the time and the inclination. Having a smart diet coupled with appropriate exercise helps with all our modern medical issues such as Type II diabetes, high blood pressure, and other circulatory issues that may lead to heart disease and stroke.

You should set up a routine and stick to it. Mine looks like this; my alarm goes off at five fifteen each morning, I get up, make a cup of coffee, and feed our cats. By five thirty I'm at the table pounding the keyboard for an hour. When I finish writing, I get some water and begin to exercise. A ten-mile mountain bike ride takes me forty-five minutes. A vigorous twenty-five-minute treadmill walk with an incline is followed up with five to ten minutes on the rower. I rotate these two cardio programs every couple of days and inject body weight and light dumbbell routines to keep my core strong.

My routine gets two key items off my personal wellness list at the beginning of my day. I love to write, and it is a form of escape and meditation for me. It flexes my mind in creative ways and it doesn't feel like problem solving. The physical training checks the health and mental distraction boxes. I don't allow myself to think about work or other challenges when I work out. I use the time to focus on my needs. Can't pack in a workout starting at five? Start at four or do it during lunch.

Meditation

When I was in my twenties, I took martial arts instruction from an interesting former Army Ranger. This instructor was a Vietnam veteran and he'd become an expert in a little-known form of Korean martial arts created in ancient times to defeat invading Chinese forces north of Korea. This style wasn't associated with competitive sports and that's why I and several other SEALs found it so attractive. It was all about gaining and maintaining a warrior mindset and achieving a mind-body readiness for battle. I ate it up!

A key part of this art was meditation. A warrior must be centered, like calm water. We were taught how to calm our heart rate by using breathing exercises while imagining our bodies going numb, feet first, then the legs, and so on. I was fascinated by the sense of control and awareness I achieved using this technique. Years later I realized meditation and breathing exercises were standard fair in not only Asia but also in India and the Middle East.

Meditation doesn't have to be lengthy or elaborate. There are hundreds of online programs, webinars, books, and actual schools where you can learn how to master your mind's turbulent attempts to solve everything, all the time. If you practice this enough you will find almost anyplace will work if all you want is a quick five-minute respite. Maybe it's not as great as a midday nap but it sure clears the cobwebs. I confess I rediscover the practice of meditation every few years or so. I strive to make it a lifelong habit, but alas, stress gets in the way.

The Critical Need for Sleep

I've always taken sleep for granted. I never had problems getting to sleep and when I do have problems it stems from getting to bed too late in the evening only to be shocked awake at five fifteen when my internal alarm goes off. There are lots of basic rules for getting a good night's sleep. Don't keep the lights on, don't leave the television on, don't live stream or binge endless content on your smart tablet while lying in bed, and don't drink alcohol before bedtime. These are prudent rules and according to most medical professionals and sleep therapists, they will help most people achieve the rest they crave.

Leaders need to sleep and sleep soundly. The brain is wired

to address threats and solve problems. If a threat is imminent or likely, the human brain will continue to work the problem, even on the subconscious level, even when asleep. Leaders are paid to deal with challenges and the challenges are rarely trivial. This means you, a leader, will have a difficult time turning it off.

I said I get to sleep easily and that's true. However, if a sound wakens me late in the night or early morning my eyes often pop open fully awake and in seconds, I'm in the middle of solving a problem at work. I don't remember my dreams, but I do recognize and remember how waking up this way feels. I win the fight to return to sleep half the time, losing ten to fifteen minutes in the process.

Half the time I do not win the battle for sleep and I need a distraction for my brain. Something to trick it into letting me disengage long enough to drop off. I use an e-book for this purpose. It's self-illuminating and set at a low brightness level. I read novels to transport my mind away from threat mitigation to a place where everything is imaginary.

If you have problems getting to sleep and staying that way for a solid eight hours, and you've tried the standard methods described above, maybe it's time to see a sleep therapist. Sleep testing, followed by sleep therapy, is the answer for many people struggling with insomnia or even mild sleep disorders. A lack of quality sleep will inhibit a leader's logical decision-making process and result in emotional, knee jerk actions inconsistent with good judgment.

The military has conducted in-depth studies for years watching how pilots lose situational awareness and mental acuity from a lack of quality sleep. An extended use of quick naps instead of a good full night's sleep, can turn a top pilot into an accident waiting to happen in a matter of days.

I've been sleep deprived in the SEALs and watched the effects on myself and others who by selection were tougher and more resilient than most. Hell Week is a sleep deprivation exercise that teaches the students the limits of performance when in a sleep deprived state. If you adopted only one of the ideas in this chapter, adopt a discipline of healthy rest.

A Life of Balance

I've only scratched the surface on wellness techniques. There are hundreds of ways to get healthy and stay that way, and lots of reasons to do so other than being a leader. I encourage you to think about your health and your daily readiness, mental and physical, to perform your leadership role. Stress can be invisible, so you need to also get yourself checked annually to make sure your stress isn't slowly killing you. I follow this advice. I've been blessed with a healthy constitution and lived a physical life longer than many my age.

My yearly physicals were boring. That is until 2017 when they discovered I had kidney cancer. I had surgery within a week and have fully recovered from that threat, but in 2020, during a routine exam, my doctor discovered skin cancer on my lower left leg. Again, it was removed and I'm good to go, but what if I hadn't been getting physicals every year? The doctors caught both cancers at the earliest possible stage of detection. Go get yourself checked and do it often. To be as effective as you can be as a leader you must also be well!

Chapter Twenty

Go Ahead, Be Nimble!

"Being nimble and ready to change our minds if need be is an attribute that is crucial to live and thrive in a society that is powered by science and technology, both as an individual and as an engaged citizen."
Priyamvada Natarajan

Being nimble, a nimble thinker, a nimble leader, isn't a destination, it's a journey. The journey begins with acceptance of where you are now, and what you must do to get where you want to go, personally and professionally. Each chapter of this book could have been a separate book and I may have only scratched the surface, but it wasn't my intent to deliver a deep academic experience. I wanted to provoke thought, even better, action.

You now have the basic tools and insights to take your leadership game to the next level. As I sat down to plan out the structure of this book, I realized there were a few core points I needed to make that I believed would resonate and provide constructive instruction to leaders and those who seek to become leaders. These simple core observations were made based on a combination of my education, experiences, and being coached and mentored by some of the best military and business minds in the country. I encourage you to go back and highlight what made sense to you and use those points to become better, to dream bigger.

I often read business books and take away ideas from twenty-five percent of the material only to come back a few years later to reread the information and find another twenty-five percent is now applicable in my current situation. This makes perfect sense. We change, we evolve, and we grow. Hold onto this book and refer to it from time to time and I assure you things you brushed over in the first reading will jump out at you later when your leadership situation has changed due to greatly increased responsibility, accountability, or both.

Living to Learn

I'm a lifelong learner. Staying humble, and a little paranoid, suits me fine. I balance my studies evenly between personal growth and professional competency. Reading to relax falls into the personal growth category as does reading or studying subjects that have nothing whatsoever to do with my business. To gain greater competency I divide my attention between topics related to my business and topics that are tangential to how I make a living.

This second professional focus is where I find the nuggets of ideas, best practices from other industries, and unique applications of technology. Studying in this way keeps me honest and alert to my everchanging intellectual surroundings. Age should not be a limiting factor for a nimble mind. You have access to the same flow of information, the same disruptive influences, that a freshly minted university student has. If you don't fall back on old habits, decide to remain humble, you will be as young as you *think*.

I've followed this self-learning discipline for many years. It's paid dividends in strange ways. Often, I find I've become acquainted or even knowledgeable about a breakthrough in other industries, only to see the utility of these approaches in my industry a year or two down the road. I don't plan for this to happen, but great ideas eventually spread and influence, disrupt, or destroy older ways of doing things. They seep across markets and industries to infect and influence adjacent zones of enterprise.

If you follow the tenets expressed in this book you should

have no problem staying on your toes, your finely tuned situational awareness keenly scanning for the next big thing, the next great opportunity, the next big threat. Learn to love learning, stay agile and stay openminded. I guarantee you will reap the benefits of this effort to stay intellectually engaged.

My Challenge to You

Now you've read this book and it's time to make some changes. Are you up to this? Can you set your mind to being nimble? Creative? Openminded? I believe you can, or I wouldn't have written this book. I mentor people, leaders, and aspiring leaders, who tell me they can't find answers by looking to academics. Leadership isn't examined in business schools in any constructive way and military leadership, while interesting, much of what is written or taught doesn't align with the very real challenges leaders face in the world.

I've tried to capture the essence of these concerns and to break out the leadership challenges or misunderstandings that are cited most often, those that have adversely affected the performance of myself and countless others. To that end I hope you've enjoyed the ride and go on to accomplish great deeds. I have faith in you and trust if you're reading this book, you're already on your way to becoming a nimble leader. Good luck and above all, *Be Nimble and be happy!*

About the Author

Marty Strong has established an accomplished military and business leadership career spanning four decades. He served twenty years as a Navy SEAL and after retiring from service, he became a successful account vice president with the United Bank of Switzerland. After seven years, Marty moved on to create a leadership consulting practice before becoming a successful senior vice president for a billion-dollar-a-year defense contracting company. In 2009, Marty joined a small, early-stage growth company, where he rose to CEO and Chief Strategy Officer over six years. Today he leads an employee-owned enterprise, consisting of three operating businesses focused on the public and private healthcare markets. *Be Nimble, How the Navy SEAL Mindset Wins on the Battlefield and in Business*, will apply Marty's considerable hands-on leadership knowledge and experience to the challenges leaders face today.

Note to Readers

Thank you for spending your hard earned money on *Be Nimble*. Even more valuable is the time you've invested in learning and gaining a professional edge. I salute your effort and your discipline! If you have a few moments, please feel free to add your review of my book to your favorite online site. Feedback is always welcome. Please visit my SAGA Performance Consulting website, http://www.martystrongbenimble.com, for news on upcoming works, recent blog posts, and to sign up for my newsletter.

Sincerely, Marty Strong

Business Books

Business Books publishes practical guides and insightful non-fiction for beginners and professionals. Covering aspects from management skills, leadership and organizational change to positive work environments, career coaching and self-care for managers, our books are a valuable addition to those working in the world of business.

15 Ways to Own Your Future
Take Control of Your Destiny in Business and in Life
Michael Khouri
A 15-point blueprint for creating better collaboration, enjoyment, and success in business and in life.
Paperback: 978-1-78535-300-0 ebook: 978-1-78535-301-7

The Common Excuses of the Comfortable Compromiser
Understanding Why People Oppose Your Great Idea
Matt Crossman
Comfortable compromisers block the way of anyone trying to change anything. This is your guide to their common excuses.
Paperback: 978-1-78099-595-3 ebook: 978-1-78099-596-0

The Failing Logic of Money

Duane Mullin

Money is wasteful and cruel, causes war, crime and dysfunctional feudalism. Humankind needs happiness, peace and abundance. So banish money and use technology and knowledge to rid the world of war, crime and poverty.

Paperback: 978-1-84694-259-4 ebook: 978-1-84694-888-6

Mastering the Mommy Track

Juggling Career and Kids in Uncertain Times

Erin Flynn Jay

Mastering the Mommy Track tells the stories of everyday working mothers, the challenges they have faced, and lessons learned.

Paperback: 978-1-78099-123-8 ebook: 978-1-78099-124-5

Modern Day Selling

Unlocking Your Hidden Potential

Brian Barfield

Learn how to reconnect sales associates with customers and unlock hidden sales potential.

Paperback: 978-1-78099-457-4 ebook: 978-1-78099-458-1

The Most Creative, Escape the Ordinary, Excel at Public Speaking Book Ever

All The Help You Will Ever Need in Giving a Speech

Philip Theibert

The 'everything you need to give an outstanding speech' book, complete with original material written by a professional speech-writer.

Paperback: 978-1-78099-672-1 ebook: 978-1-78099-673-8

On Business And For Pleasure

A Self-Study Workbook for Advanced Business English

Michael Berman

This workbook includes enjoyable challenges and has been designed to help students with the English they need for work.

Paperback: 978-1-84694-304-1

Small Change, Big Deal

Money as if People Mattered

Jennifer Kavanagh

Money is about relationships: between individuals and between communities. Small is still beautiful, as peer lending model, micro-credit, shows.

Paperback: 978-1-78099-313-3 ebook: 978-1-78099-314-0